leisure &

Licence

Andrea Clegg

Clink
Street

London | New York

Published by Clink Street Publishing 2016

Copyright © 2016

First edition.

ISBN: 978-1-910782-87-3
E-Book: 978-1-910782-88-0

Preface

This book is intended to be a practical and helpful guide to general motorists. Since setting up my business in Road Traffic Defence people have been asking questions about motoring law. It is apparent from their questions that many make decisions about whether to accept a fixed penalty ticket or a summons based on misconceptions, many of which are wrong e.g. the police will not prosecute below 10mph over the speed limit.

I have researched reader's views of the very few road traffic guidance books available and it is clear that readers want a combination of both accurate law and a simple clear guide as to how to deal with the matter if they wanted to represent themselves at any stage. They want to know how to fight a case if necessary.

Whilst some circumstances will warrant instructing specialist lawyers, such as my firm, Auriga Advocates Ltd, it is the more expensive option and is more appropriate for those with the money and motivation to pay someone to represent them. For example, if an individual was likely to be disqualified or may, if they attended court, lose money in their time, and thus it is more cost effective to pay a lawyer to represent them.

The reality is that there are many prosecutions which are

unjustified and merely accepted by motorists. The system is now prosecuted by the police who in some areas offer advice to the defendant, thus playing the role of prosecutor and defender. The police will undoubtedly have targets, one of which will be the early disposal of a case i.e. plea and dealt with on the first hearing. In my view there is a clear conflict and I would question the independence and the quality of the advice being given as a result It appears to me that most defendants will take the advice, firstly because it is free and secondly because they do not think that the police would mislead them. In my view, it is in the interests of the police to persuade a defendant to plead guilty, and from my own experience at court they do not advise defendants to seek independent legal advice, even when defendants are expressing concern about the advice being given.

It is important to understand the disparity between the prosecution and the defence in these circumstances, because whilst the prosecution can approach defendants to give them advice, the defence cannot, and have to wait until they are approached. Even if we were to overhear the wrong advice being given by a prosecutor, we could not approach that defendant offering to provide him with the correct advice.

I feel that motorists are poorly guided and represented. Their position is getting more and more onerous as the government authorises the issuing of fixed penalty notices for more offences, i.e. driving without due care and attention (August 2013) – quite wrongly, in my view.

As the roads get busier and more regulations are brought in and enforced, the motorist will suffer if they do not improve their legal knowledge.

You will have heard of "Mr Loophole"; in my view there are very few loopholes. It is the practice of understanding the law, testing the prosecution evidence and preparing a thorough defence which can result in getting you off an offence. Often it is the lack of following procedure which provides a way out of an offence for a motorist, and the only way of testing this is to get disclosure of the evidence, which is all too often too little in motoring offences, as the prosecution only provide basic disclosure.

I hope that by reading this and retaining it as a reference you will be better equipped to deal with motoring issues which you may face; and if after reading it, you feel you would benefit from some legal advice, contact Auriga Advocates for free no-obligation advice or a specialist of your choice.

I hope you enjoy my book and I wish you happy and prosecution-free motoring.

Andrea Clegg
Senior Solicitor/Managing Director
Auriga Advocates Ltd
www.roadtrafficdefencelawyers.co.uk

Table of Contents

- No MOT
- Forgery, False Statements And Producing False Documents
- Driving Whilst Disqualified
- Procedure When Stopped By A Police Officer
- Procedure When Summonsed

- Provisional Licence Holders
- Supervisors
- New Drivers

- Notice Of Intended Prosecution
- Driver Information Requests

- Types Of Road
- Speed Limit Signs
- Temporary Speed Limits
- Motorway Speed Limits
- Vehicle Speed Limits
- Speed Check Methods
- Fixed Camera
- Laser
- Radar
- Vascar

Appendices

Chapter One
Road Traffic Courses

National Drivers Improvement Scheme

Many motorists are offered driver improvement courses as an alternative to prosecution for certain offences.

Motorists may be offered one of the following courses:

1. Speed Awareness
2. Driver Alertness
3. What's Driving Us
4. Driving4Change

Each course is offered in a case at the discretion of a police officer who follows ACPO (Association of Chief Policers) Guidelines issued in 2012 known as NDORS, which stands for the National Driver Offender Retraining Scheme. These are all offered as an alternative to prosecution, unlike the Drink Driver Rehabilitation Course which is specifically offered to convicted drink drivers.

The concept of driver retraining was introduced by Dr P North as far back as 1988, but not adopted by the government until much later. Dr P North believed that there was little evidence to show that punishing offenders raised standards in motorists driving and that retraining was more likely to bring about improvement in their driving, particularly if the retraining concentrated on the shortcomings in their driving.

This is now reflected in the courses mentioned above which I will deal with in turn.

Speed Awareness

A speed awareness course can be offered if a motorist's speed is within a range of 10% + 2 to 10% + 9 above the speed limit. This does not apply to 20mph speed limit zones. If speed is a key factor in an incident where there has been a collision, a motorist should be offered the Driver Alertness Course.

The course costs £80-£100 depending on the course provider. The course runs for 4 hours and is classroom based; however, there is a practical option which can be added which will extend the course to 5 hours.

TABLE OF SPEED LIMIT GUIDELINES FOR RECOMMENDING SPEED AWARENESS COURSE

Limit	Device Tolerance	Speed Awareness From	To
20mph	22mph	24mph	31mph
30mph	32 mph	35mph	42mph
40mph	42mph	46mph	53mph
50mph	52mph	57mph	64mph
60mph	62mph	68mph	75mph
70mph	73mph	79mph	86mph

Driver Alertness

This can be offered to a motorist who is involved in a road traffic accident where there has been a collision and it would justify a S3 (driving without due care and attention or inconsiderate driving (post)) prosecution. The decision to offer the course should be made on the failing in the motorist's driving, and not the consequences of that failing, although there is some consideration to the consequences if they are so serious that they would justify a prosecution i.e. life threatening injuries, fatality or permanent disability.

The course costs £125-£200 depending on the course provider. The course runs for 6 hours and includes both classroom and practical driving sessions.

What's Driving Us

This course can be offered where a motorist makes an act or omission in driving which does not involve a collision. The aim is to correct the mischief, intentional or deliberate act done by the motorist. It is for offences such as using a mobile phone whilst driving, or not being in a position to have proper control, which might attract this sort of course. If there is a high risk of a collision or harm then the police are unlikely to offer this course.

The course costs £80-£100. It is classroom based and lasts 3.25 hours.

Driving 4 Change

This course can be offered when a motorist makes minor error in judgement or has a lapse in concentration, or otherwise demonstrates a lack of awareness as to the law or the wider consequences of his/her actions.

You must be able to read a number plate with or without glasses in good daylight at a distance of 20.5 metres (67 feet), or 20 metres (65 feet) if it is a new style number plate.

You must be the holder of a full driving licence.

The course will costs £80-£100 depending on the provider. It lasts two and a quarter hours and is a practical course.

NDORS provides general guidance to police offers about what they should take into account:

1. The circumstances of the incident, which will be things such as the time of day, presence of other motorists, risk of collision or injury to name but a few.

2. Any other additional evidence which may be evidence pertaining to the motorist.

3. The defendant's explanation.

4. Before deciding to prosecute, as opposed to offering the course, they should apply the CPS full code test for charging, which means there should be evidence of the offence and it is in the public interest to prosecute.

I have dealt with thousands of motoring offences and motorists and it is rare to see an officer make any detailed note of a defendant's explanation. Surprisingly, they often only give the briefest details of the circumstances and insufficient to establish any clear mitigating factors or aggravating factors. So if you are reported for an offence, you should always make a note of the circumstances, which may be useful mitigation, and you should always write to the police traffic process department with an explanation and surrounding circumstances if you feel that you would qualify for one of the courses mentioned above.

Before the police can offer any course, there must be:-

- Realistic prospect of conviction
- No other offences
- A similar course must not have been taken within the previous three years
- The defendant must be a holder of a current driving licence or competence certificate to drive or ride.

The defendant/driver MUST:-
- Accept to pay the fee
- Abide by the terms and conditions of the course provider
- Complete the course and accept that records will be kept.

It is important to note that you will not be allowed a second chance if you have "no reasonable excuse for non-compliance" (6.2) so if you are running late or unable to attend, it is imperative that you contact the provider and offer a reasonable excuse, quoting the guidance, so that they will offer you another course. If you fail to do this you will be prosecuted for the offence.

It is not true to say that once you are prosecuted you cannot be offered the course. The regulations only enable the police or the CPS to authorise the course, so if you leave it until a court hearing and ask the court, they will be unable to remit the matter back to the police. It is always better to make your representations to the police, or as a last resort to the CPS; if they indicate that the decision has been made to prosecute and it is too late, you should point out that under the guidelines the CPS can make the decision and that the police did not properly take into account all the factors which have been mentioned above.

As a prosecutor for many years I often referred cases back to the police for a defendant to take a course if the circumstances justified that course of action under the guidelines. The matter before the court would then be adjourned until confirmation of completing the course was received, at which time I would then withdraw the proceedings or discontinue the case.

It is not the decision of the police officer who stops you to make the decision, but he should note any explanation you offer and make a full note of all the surrounding circumstances which may influence that decision. The case is then reviewed by a supervisor who will make the decision to either offer the course or prosecute.

When dealing with the police officer at the scene, co-operate fully and calmly offer your explanation to him. Thereafter make a note of what you have said and put it in writing to the police, as you will not be certain that the officer will be have noted your explanation in full. Then you will be able to send representations in based on the information you gave to the police officer.

MOTORCYCLISTS

Motorcyclists make up about 1% of the motoring population but account for a disproportionate level of serious injury and fatalities. This is thought to be due to two factors: firstly, other motorists being unaware of the presence of motorcyclists, but also the exposed nature of motorcycling and often the mindset of certain motorcyclists.

RIDE (Riders Intervention Developing Experience)

RIDE was developed out of the Driver Improvement Scheme to offer motorcyclists a specialist training course which deals specifically with the sort of issues that motorcyclists have, which are often extremely different to those of the car driver.

The course is offered when the motorcyclist has demonstrated adrenalin-fuelled riding, where the rider is chasing the thrill of dangerous manoeuvres, or riding in areas which are inappropriate for anti-social riding and low level careless riding.

It is not available for speed camera-detected speeding or speeding in general; such motorcyclists would be offered the Speed Awareness Course.

The aim is not to restrict motorcyclists, but to reduce the level of accidents and motorcyclist casualties.

DRINK DRIVE REHABILITATION COURSE

This course is designed for defendants who have been convicted of a drink/drug drive offence and have been disqualified for a period of 12 months or more. It covers drink drive offences and related offences such as "in charge", "attempting to drive", failure to provide a specimen, and causing death by drink driving.

The Magistrates at sentence will offer the course and in general you will get up to 25% reduction in the overall disqualification.

DISQUALIFICATION	REDUCTION
12 months	3 months
16 months	4 months
24 months	6 months
36 months	9 months

The course is a three day course and will cost between £110 (with concessions) and £175. Prices will vary on whether you qualify for concessions and whether you wish to attend on weekdays or the weekend.

Research has shown 17% of people who do not attend a course commit another drink driving offence within a 6 year period, compared with only 7% of those who do attend a course.

Attending the course has advantages; although it will cost money, it can ultimately reduce insurance costs, which can increase dramatically if you are convicted for drink driving.

Chapter Two
Fixed Penalty Tickets

Fixed penalty tickets, known as fixed penalty notices (FPN), are a popular and quick way of the government punishing defendants and also recouping fines. However, they can hold numerous pitfalls for the motorist. An FPN can only be issued if a motorist fulfils the following criteria:-

1. The motorist holds a driving licence

2. The motorist will not be subject to the "totting up" procedure ie 12 points or more on licence after adding the points for the offence

3. The motorist must be able to surrender his licence for endorsement.

If a motorist is unable to fulfil the criteria the officer will report the motorist for summons. The officer does have discretion as to whether to report an individual or not, and the less serious the driving incident, the less likely that the officer will report that individual for the offence.

If summonsed, there are additional costs, however there are ways a motorist can reduce these to reflect a fixed penalty fee.

It is important that when stopped by an officer that you follow these simple guidelines:-

1. Always co-operate and be polite to the officer as the more co-operative and polite you are, the more likely it is that the officer will exercise discretion in your favour.

2. Always make a note of the traffic conditions including weather, road surface, level of traffic, pedestrians, visibility and any other prevailing factors which would have an impact on either the reason for the manner of your driving, or the risk your driving posed to others or their property.

3. You may offer an explanation for your driving and if you are offering a true and honest explanation it is safe to do so, but do not try to make excuses which are not founded, and do not rely on the officer making a note of what you say; you must make a note of your explanation to the officer. If in any doubt at all, say nothing at all and just accept the procedure politely.

DO NOT:

1. Lose your temper with the officer or start arguing with him.

2. Insult the police officer in any way as this may result in more serious criminal charges.

3. Do not rip up any documents the officer gives you, as this is the only police evidence you will have of the incident, so it is vital that you retain all documentation.

4. Do NOT admit liability at the scene. ALWAYS accept the documentation and seek legal advice. Auriga Advocates offer free, independent no-obligation initial advice and this is the same for most firms specialising in road traffic law.

In order to issue an FPN legally, the officer must be a constable in uniform. The only exception to this is in relation to auto detection devices, such as the fixed speed cameras. You should always note the officer's name and collar number, along with whether or not he was in uniform and if he was with anyone else, including another police officer.

ACPO GUIDELINES FOR SPEEDS AT WHICH OFFICERS SHOULD ISSUE A FIXED PENALTY OR SUMMONS

Speed Limit	Speed for FPN	Speed for Summons
20mph	24mph	35mph
30mph	35mph	50mph
40mph	46mph	56mph
50mph	57mph	76mph
60mph	68mph	86mph
70mph	79mph	96mph

Note that these are guidelines only, and the issuing of a FPN is always at the discretion of an officer, assuming of course that you fulfil the criteria mentioned above.

TRAFFIC OFFICER REPORT

An officer may report you for process and issue a traffic officer report (TOR) which delays the decision as to whether to prosecute, issue a fixed penalty or offer a retraining course. This decision is made in the traffic process office and, as they have to take into account any explanation offered to them, it would provide you with the chance to provide your explanation and influence the decision.

You could get a letter of representation written by an expert to influence the decision at this stage. Auriga Advocates offer such services from £200, other firms may charge more.

FIXED PENALTY CONDITIONAL OFFER

This relates to authorised automatic detection offences such as fixed speed cameras etc., so that an FPN would not be issued to the driver or secured on the vehicle at the time, and the procedure has to follow a strict criteria:

The conditional offer must contain:-

1. The particulars of the offence so that a driver can understand which incident the offer relates to

2. The amount of the fixed penalty for the offence; and

3. A statement that proceedings against the alleged offender cannot be commenced in respect of that offence until the end of the period of 28 days following the date on which the conditional offer was issued (a longer period may be specified in the offer).

Otherwise the same conditions apply as to other fixed penalty notices.

ACPO GUIDELINES FOR CARELESS AND INCONSIDERATE DRIVING

REPORT/CONDITIONAL OFFER/FIXED PENALTY NOTICE/COURSE

These are restricted to offences which are only observed by police officers and there are no victims, no collisions and no public complaint. It covers but is not restricted to the following types of driving.

• Lower level aggressive and inconsiderate driving where others are not unduly affected
• Driving too close to the vehicle in front
• Failing to give way at a junction causing no evasive action by another driver
• Overtaking and forcing into a queue of traffic
• Using the wrong lane on a roundabout
• Ignoring a lane closed sign and forcing into a queue of traffic
• Poor lane discipline i.e. remaining in lane two or three when lane one is empty
• Inappropriate speed i.e. too slow
• Wheel spins
• Handbrake turns

REPORT/SUMMONS

These cover situations which may be observed by an officer alone but will cover those with civilians, witnesses and collisions. It covers but is not restricted to following types of driving:

• Aggressive driving where others are endangered or have to take real evasive action

• Fast overtakes and lane hopping/weaving with other drivers having to evade

• Pulling out in front of other moving vehicle that needs to brake

• Overtaking and causing the approaching vehicle to brake or take evading action

• Pulling in causing the overtaken vehicle to brake or swerve

• Wrong lane on roundabout causing another vehicle on the roundabout to brake or swerve

• Staying in lane two or three with vehicles behind being held up or forced to pass on the nearside

FIXED PENALTY NOTICES - NON ENDORSABLE DRIVER NOT PRESENT

Different rules apply to fixed penalty notices which are issued and usually stuck on the vehicle, i.e. parking offences. These are non-endorseable. No offences will be commenced until after a period of 21 days (the police will not commence proceedings on these types of offences until the lapse of 28 days).

For the purposes of these fixed penalty tickets, it is assumed that the registered keeper is the owner, but a person can produce a statement of ownership stating that he was never the owner or when ownership changed.

If you do not respond to a notice at all and the penalty remains unpaid, then the penalty will increase by 50% as a fine which is registered. A notice of registration will then be issued, but it is possible to provide a declaration to show that you did not receive the initial notice, you were not the owner at the time or that you gave a notice requesting a hearing.

It is always worth acting on these notices immediately; if it is a parking notice and there are circumstances that you feel would make you not guilty, you should do the following:

1. Take photographs of any restrictions and exceptions displayed
2. Take photographs of loads etc.
3. Keep copies of any documentation you have in relation to why you were present
4. Make notes of all the circumstance including times of arrival and departure etc.

It is worth contacting a specialist motoring firm who can give you free advice regarding the best way forward with these types of offences, and if disputed, could write to the relevant authority in your defence – there would be a charge for this.

It is important to seek advice because many private companies produce tickets which closely resemble penalty notices, and the procedure is very different, as is the likelihood of avoiding the penalty.

Note that it is an offence to interfere or damage a fixed penalty notice which has not been issued to you. This is a level 5 fine, which is unlimited for offences after the 12th March 2015 otherwise £5,000.

I HAVE BEEN GIVEN A FIXED PENALTY - WHAT DO I DO NOW?

Once issued with an FPN, you will have 28 days in which to respond so it is vital that you seek advice from a specialist solicitor such as Auriga Advocates well within 28 days. If you are advised that you should be pleading guilty, you should respond to the FPN sending in your driving licence (if not already surrendered) and the fine within the deadline given. If you fail, a summons will be issued and there will be an increase in costs and the fine imposed.

If you have a genuine and reasonable excuse for being unable to accept the fixed penalty, sometimes you can persuade the Magistrates to impose the rate of the fixed penalty notice – however, this will usually be the case where the circumstances for being unable to be dealt with under the fixed penalty notice procedure were beyond your control. If you change your address from the one given to the police officer, it is your responsibility to inform the police so that they can keep you up to date; the Magistrates are unlikely to accept that you were unable to respond to the fixed penalty because you failed to tell the police your new address.

It is always worth considering, if you are likely to receive a high fine and costs, either writing an explanation to the court or paying a specialist solicitor to write a letter in mitigation, which is more likely to persuade Magistrates to reduce your fine and points or sentence you to a fixed penalty rate.

If you have sought advice and wish to plead not guilty, you should respond to the fixed penalty with a not guilty plea and a summons will be issued for court proceedings; the same would occur if you just ignored the summons.

For information on the types of offences for which the police can issue a fixed penalty ticket and the fine rates, please refer to Appendix 1.

The information regarding any possible endorsement of points on your licence, or the possible imposition of a disqualification, will be contained on the documentation sent to you by the police. You will not be offered a fixed penalty ticket if you may be disqualified for the offence, or under the "totting up" procedure.

POLICE POWERS TO STOP

The police have the power to stop any vehicle for any reason. Once they have stopped you, they can request production of your driving documents i.e. your driving licence, insurance certificate and your MOT if required. If you cannot produce them, they will usually issue you with a HORT/ 1 which will detail which documents you need to produce within 7 days to a police station of your choice. You should always inform officers if you are unable to do so that they can extend the period on the HORT/1. This extension is not possible for fixed penalty tickets.

There are regulations which govern what the police are allowed to do in certain offences and how the police are allowed to deal with a motorist, such as not being allowed to stop a motorist at random to undertake a breathe test. These are dealt with in the relevant chapters.

APPENDIX 1 Fixed Penalty offences.

Chapter Three
No Insurance, No Driving Licence and No MOT

DRIVING WITHOUT INSURANCE

If you are using a motor vehicle on a road you must have valid insurance. It is also an offence to permit or cause the driving of a vehicle without insurance. You must have an insurance policy in force and you must comply with the conditions of that insurance. It will not be a defence that you did not know just because you did not read your policy.

Most insurance policies have restrictive conditions:-

- Who is permitted to use the vehicle
- What vehicles can be used
- How old the driver must be, particularly on the condition enabling the policy holder to drive other vehicles i.e. 25 years of age.
- What the vehicle is used for i.e. social and domestic purposes only
- The vehicle is not to be used for hire or reward.

When taking out a policy you must ensure that you explain who is going to drive the vehicle and all the purposes it will be used for, i.e. driving for work purposes, as this will change the standard conditions and probably add a condition "for business use". It will be a little more expensive but not as expensive as a penalty for driving without insurance if you fail to ensure the policy covers the purpose for use.

Examples of business use:-

- Window cleaners
- Landscape gardeners
- Builders
- Take-away deliveries
- Use at work to travel between places of work

It is important to declare any type of use you may have for your vehicle whilst at work, no matter how minor the use is. If you are found not to have business cover for your vehicle under these circumstances, you will not only be convicted of driving without insurance and receive a fine and between 6 and 8 points on your licence, you are likely to have your vehicle seized by the police. This will cost in the region of

£150-250 to get released, depending on where you live.

New drivers will have the same issues as above but also, because the offence incurs 6 points, they will have the added implication of the new driver provisions which – due to the imposition of 6 points – will result in their licence reverting back to a provisional status, so effectively the driver will be a learner driver, which is even more expensive and inconvenient.

Driving Licence Condition On Insurance

Most insurance companies will ask the driver if they hold a driving licence or have held a driving licence and is not disqualified. In these cases unless the policy says otherwise, the insurance will cover you if the driving licence has expired. If it is not mentioned in a policy then even if you do not have a licence, or are disqualified, you will be covered by the insurance until such time as the insurance company void the insurance. This cannot be backdated, so only runs from the time and date that the insurance is cancelled or voided.

Care should be taken as insurance companies tend to put a clause into the policy stating that the policyholder or named driver must hold a current driving licence or have held a current driving licence and not be disqualified, and in these cases you will be breaching a condition of the insurance policy which will void the insurance from the start, so you would not be covered. The policy must be specific so unless it specifies otherwise, licence would include a foreign driving licence.

Most insurance policies state that the vehicle must not be used for hire or reward, although sharing or using a vehicle and just paying for the petrol will not fall foul of this condition. If there is any profit in the use of the vehicle in these circumstances, it will usually be classed as using for hire or reward and will fall foul of this condition.

The onus of proof is on the "user" to check and never take a person's word that you will be insured, and many drivers have assumed they will be covered but have not checked their policy. Always check policies before driving a new vehicle or someone else's.

A regular condition is that the policy owner will be covered to drive another vehicle not owned by the policy holder, so if you purchased a second vehicle, unless you are covered for two vehicles you own, you will be required to take out second insurance on the second vehicle because your current policy will usually not cover you.

Many drivers fall foul of the "no insurance" offences by failing to check that premiums are being paid if they pay by direct debit. Often direct debits are not honoured and the insurance company cancel the policy; as the offence is one of strict liability, you will still be guilty of driving without insurance but may have special reasons for non-endorsement if you have a good reason as to why you would have been unaware of the cancellation. Most insurance companies will make it clear in the documentation that non-payment of premiums will result in the policy being cancelled, so arguments that you were unaware because you failed to read your documentation, or that you did not notice the lack of payment on your statement, is unlikely to be a good reason as the court will expect you to have exercised all due diligence.

I have dealt with the odd rare case where a policyholder's insurance was cancelled erroneously on the basis of non-payment of the premium when the insurance company had continued to take all the monthly premiums, thus the cancellation was wrong. Nevertheless, the driver was driving without insurance; as he had entered a plea of not guilty, he was too late to make representations to the police to withdraw the charge altogether, but he was technically uninsured. However, I was able to persuade the court to give him an absolute discharge without endorsement and no costs. Such cases are rare.

Most motorists think that the offence is driving without insurance, but the words in the legislation are "use", "permit" and "cause".

Use

"Use" covers using the vehicle for any reason. Parking outside your house on the road would be an offence. Travelling as a passenger in your own vehicle uninsured would be an offence of using. This would not, as many think, be "permitting", because by being a passenger the vehicle is being used for your benefit.

Permit

"Permitting" is allowing someone to use a vehicle without insurance. The only time you would not be permitting is if you made it a pre-condition that the person had to have insurance or a driving licence.

Cause

"Causing" requires knowledge of the facts which makes the use of a vehicle unlawful, i.e. an employer instructs an employee to take a vehicle out knowing that it has defective tyres, or allows the employee to drive the vehicle knowing that he does not hold the requisite licence. This would not apply to insurance, because an employer is almost always using the vehicle as it is being used for the benefit of the employer.

Under S143(3) there is a defence for employees charged with using a vehicle without insurance. The conditions for this defence are:-

a) the vehicle did not belong to the defendant and was not in his possession under hire/loan

b) it was being used in the course of his employment AND

c) he neither knew nor had reason to believe that there was no insurance policy in force for his use of the vehicle.

The burden of proof for the defence is on the defendant on a balance of probabilities.

The penalty for using, permitting or causing a vehicle to be used without insurance carries a hefty penalty with a level 5 fine of £5,000 (unlimited from the 12th March 2015), 6-8 points and discretionary disqualification which is likely to be imposed if there is evidence of sustained use of a vehicle without insurance, or a serious accident has occurred and the defendant is at fault.

APPENDIX 2 Sentencing guidelines for No Insurance

S154(1) of the Road Traffic Act 1988 creates an obligation on a person against whom a claim is being made to state:

• Whether or not he was insured or would have been insured except for the insurance cancelling the policy, and

• Particulars of that insurance as in the insurance certificate, and

• If no insurance certificate is available, the registration mark or other identifying features of vehicle or the number of the insurance policy, or such other information which will identify the insurance policy issued and the period the insurance covered. The penalty for not complying is a level 4 fine of £2,500.

KEEPING A VEHICLE WITHOUT INSURANCE

This is a new offence which was introduced by the Road Traffic Act 2006, creating S144Aof the Road Traffic Act 1988. A registered keeper of a motor vehicle who does not meet the insurance requirements will be guilty of an offence, the penalty is a level 3 fine of £1,000.

The exceptions are:
• Vehicles owned by police authorities, councils, the health services and other government departments.
• Stolen vehicles
• Former keeper has completed a SORN. (Statutory Off the Road Notice)

In order to avoid liability under this section it is important to ensure that, if you take a vehicle off the road, you complete a SORN, and if you sell/scrap the vehicle, that you notify the DVLA immediately. The fact that you may not have known about the offence will not be a defence.

New Driver Insurance

There are many issues which can arise with learner drivers and new drivers when it comes to insurance cover. It is often inexpensive to put a learner driver on a current policy, as the learner driver will usually be supervised. However, the difficulty arises when the learner passes and becomes a new driver, as premiums shoot through the roof and the temptation is very high to carry on with the policy as it is. This would mean that the new driver is not insured, and as no insurance carries a minimum of 6 points, he would revert back to being a learner driver with fines, costs, and the added costs of re-taking his test etc... As well as that, the parent could also face the charge of permitting no insurance, and receive points and a fine. Not informing the insurance company of any change is, in fact, the more expensive option in the long run. If you have misinformed the insurance company there are also other offences to consider which carry heavier penalties, such as obtaining insurance by deception.

Another point to raise with learner drivers and new drivers is that they must comply with the conditions of their licence, and with the insurance in terms of supervision and displaying plates etc. Failing to do so may render their insurance void.

Motor Insurance Bureau

Where a person who is responsible for an accident is uninsured, cannot be traced or where an insurance company has gone into liquidation, the Motor Insurance Bureau (MIB) covers personal injury and damage claims. You must make a claim within three years.

The contact address is:

MIB
Linford Wood House
6-12 Capital Drive
Linford Wood
Milton Keynes
MK14 6 XT
Website: http://www.mib.org.uk

NO DRIVING LICENCE

S87 of the Road Traffic Act 1988 requires that any person driving a motor vehicle on a road does so in accordance with a licence authorising him to drive a motor vehicle of that class. The penalty is level 3 fine of £1000 at Band A, 3-6 points and discretionary disqualification if there is no entitlement to hold a driving licence, or you are underage or not complying with the conditions of the licence, such as no L plates and unsupervised, or a learner motorcyclist carrying a passenger. The offence is not endorseable if the driver is entitled to hold a driving licence but does not have one in his possession, for example he has lost it or not applied for one after a period of disqualification.

The prosecution only have to prove that the driver was driving the vehicle; the onus is on the driver to prove he held a driving licence. (S101 MCA 1980) It is also an offence to "cause or permit" someone to drive a vehicle otherwise than in accordance with a driving licence. An employer will be held liable if he has no system to ensure that the driver has a valid driving licence and maintains a valid driving licence through his employment, so it is important as an employer that renewal dates are noted and actioned. Care should also be taken by people supervising learner drivers, because if they do not ensure that the learner driver is complying with the conditions of a provisional licence, i.e. displaying L plates, the supervisor will also be charged with an offence of causing the offence and potentially causing or permitting no insurance.

A foreign driver is usually entitled to drive on his permit, provided he is resident in Great Britain and is not disqualified from driving, for a period of one year, after which time he must apply for a full British driving licence. The best advice for a foreign driver is to apply for his full licence and take his

his driving test as soon as he gets residency in Great Britain, because this will prevent the possibility of being unable to drive legally whilst he awaits a British driving licence.

On receipt of your driving licence you must sign it immediately, as not to do so is an offence. This also applies to failing to keep your details up to date on your driving licence, such as a change of address.

Driving licence changes

Since the 8th June 2014 the paper part of a driving licence is no longer valid and is not issued by the DVLA. The "old" paper licences are still valid until such time as they are submitted for alteration, but the details for an offence will no longer be written on them by the court. The court will only require the card part of the licence in future.

Details of any offences committed will be retained by the DVLA electronically and access to this information can be obtained online, by phone or by post.

You can find this information at the following website link: **https://www.gov.uk/view-driving-licence**

However, it would be useful if you always keep your own record of any offences committed.

Renewal of Driving licences

The current driving licences come in two parts: a photo card and a paper licence. The photo card must be renewed every 10 years to provide an accurate picture of the licence holder. Under S99 of the RTA 1988, a full or provisional licence is in most circumstances valid until the holder is 70 years of age. After the age of 70, the licence must be renewed every three years. This is achieved by completing a self-declaration of fitness.

The rules are different for PCV LGV and HGV licences. LGV and PCV licences will be valid until the holder's 45th birthday and thereafter must be renewed every five years; after their 66th birthday it must be renewed annually, with a submission of a medical examination.

Appendix 3 Driving Licence Offence Codes and Endorsements

Appendix 4 Categories and Sub-categories of Vehicles for Licensing Purposes

Seizure of Your Vehicle

Under S165A, a vehicle which is being driven without insurance or otherwise than in accordance with a driving licence may be seized by the police and removed. The police have the power to enter premises in order to seize a vehicle, but this does not extend to private dwelling houses.

No MOT

All vehicles are required to be issued with an MOT certificate if they are being used on a road and are over three years of age. It is an offence to use a vehicle on a road without a valid MOT or cause or permit a vehicle the same.

The offence is not endorseable but carries a level 3 fine of £1000 or a level 4 fine if the vehicle is adapted to carry more than 8 passengers.

If the vehicle is not registered with the DVLA, i.e. a foreign vehicle, then the three year period is calculated from the date of manufacture.

Some vehicles require a MOT certificate after 12 months:

• Motor vehicle used for the carriage of people with more than 8 seats excluding the drivers
- Taxis
- Ambulances
- Large goods vehicles.

There are exceptions that allow vehicles to be used on a road:

• Taking a vehicle to and from an approved testing station for a test to be done by prior arrangement. Note prior arrangement is essential and the onus is on the driver to establish that there was a prior arrangement, so always secure a record of your appointment booking.
• When a vehicle has failed a test and it is being taken to a garage for the relevant work to be done. Again this must be by prior appointment.
• When a vehicle has failed a test and is being towed to a scrap yard.
• Police vehicles, if maintained by an approved police workshop
• Vehicles temporarily in Britain.

Forgery, false statements and producing false documents

It is an offence for anyone to forge any driving documents such as a driving licence, MOT or insurance certificate. It is also an offence to obtain any these documents by supplying false information.

It is an offence to produce a document with the intention of deceiving the recipient into believing that the contents are true when you know they are false. This could apply to producing forged documents, but also to producing documents in someone else's name and giving the police that person's name.

The offences all carry custodial penalties of up to two years.

You could also face charges of obstruct or perverting the course of justice if you provide false details to the police. The more serious offence is perverting the course of justice, which will usually be charged if, as a result of providing false details or documents, another person has been charged with an offence.

Driving Whilst Disqualified

Under S103 of the RTA 1988, it is an offence to drive whilst disqualified from holding or obtaining a driving licence or to obtain a driving licence. If a driving licence is obtained it will be totally ineffectual.

The prosecution have to prove that you were driving on a road and that you were disqualified. They can prove the disqualification by a Certificate of Memorandum, which is obtained from the court which disqualified him. The prosecution could seek to rely on a confession, but this is unreliable as often the driver can be mistaken about a disqualification. If you are stopped, it is always better to be on the safe side and not confirm that you are definitely disqualified, unless you have seen evidence to confirm your opinion that you are in fact disqualified. I have had many cases where the driver has been mistaken and is, in fact, not disqualified at all.

It is not unusual for drivers to be disqualified in their

absence and the lack of knowledge about the disqualification will not be a defence to the offence of disqualified driving. However, the prosecution do have to prove that you were the person who was disqualified. They can do this by calling someone present at the court if you attended, or with evidence from the police officer who stopped you for the offence for which you were disqualified.

The penalty is a level 5 fine of £5,000 (unlimited from the 12th March 2015) and up to 6 months' imprisonment.

Once the disqualification period has expired, the driver can apply for a driving licence, although once the application is made to the DVLA the driver can drive lawfully assuming he has relevant insurance and MOT etc. It is advisable to wait until you are in receipt of the licence. If the application is erred in any way, this will mean that you have not made a correct application and therefore you will not be entitled to drive. You have no way of knowing whether the application has been received unless you contact them directly to ask.

Note that if you are disqualified until a "re-test" is taken, you are entitled to hold a provisional driving licence but not a full driving licence. If you either drive without a provisional driving licence or you drive with a provisional licence but do not comply with the conditions, i.e. no L plates or unsupervised, you will be charged with driving whilst disqualified.

PROCEDURE WHEN STOPPED BY THE POLICE

The police have the power to stop a motorist and require the driver to produce driving documents. If they are not available at the time of being stopped, the driver will have 7 days to produce them at a station of his choice. The police officer will issue the driver with a form known as a HORT/1 which will have the details of the driver, vehicle, road, date and time, and will indicate which documents should be produced. At police station, a HORT/2 will be completed and the driver will usually be given a verbal notice of intended prosecution for any offences which come to light.

PROCEDURE IF SUMMONED FOR OFFENCES

If offences have come to light and you have not been issued with a fixed penalty notice, you will have been reported for summons. You will receive a summons (postal requisition) which will detail the offences, date, time and court to which you are summoned. For specified offences the police now prosecute, so any information required will have to be sought from the police. Details of the relevant department will be on the documentation.

There should be a summary of the offence and a plea document which will ask you to indicate your plea to the offences, with space for you to write your mitigation. You can alternatively get an expert road traffic solicitor to write a letter of mitigation for you, so you would not need to send anything back to the court as the solicitors would do everything for you. This is advisable if you are likely to receive a serious sentence such as disqualification or imprisonment. The cost varies; Auriga Advocates charge £200-300 but many others cost more.

As you are summoned, you do not have to attend court and your case can be dealt with in your absence. The plea form which you have completed will be read to the court so the court will have your mitigation. A word of caution if you are "totting" or are likely to be disqualified, or the offence carries imprisonment: my advice would be to attend, because the court may disqualify in your absence and if you continue driving you will be committing the offence of driving whilst disqualified, which carries severe penalties. If the court considers imprisonment, you will be bailed to attend court as they are unable to sentence a person to imprisonment in their absence. Thereafter if you fail to attend court, a warrant will be issued for your arrest and there will be a further offence of failing to answer court bail.

Further details about how to deal with the summons and the court procedure can be found in Chapter 16.

Chapter Four
Provisional Licence Holders, Supervisors and New Drivers

Provisional Licence Holders

Learner drivers must hold a provisional driving licence before they drive. A learner driver can obtain a provisional licence to drive a car from the age of 17 and the provisional licence will usually be valid until their 70th birthday, after which time it will have to be renewed every three years. The provisional licences for mopeds and motorcycles last for two years.

Once in receipt of a provisional licence a learner driver is able to drive a car as long as the following conditions are met:

- must be supervised by a qualified driver
- must display "L" plates ("D" in Wales).

It is an offence to fail to observe one or both of these conditions (S87 Road Traffic Act 1988). The penalty is a Level 3 fine of £1,000 and 3-6 penalty points.

Failure to observe these conditions may also result in the driver being uninsured and it may also impact on the supervisor.

Learner Drivers Of Mopeds/Motorcycles

A learner driver may ride a moped if over the age of 16 years and holding a provisional moped licence.

A moped is a motor vehicle which:

- Has an engine capacity not exceeding 50cc
- Does not weigh more than 250kg
- Has a design maximum speed of 50kph (31mph).

(S108(1) of the RTA 1988)

A learner is not allowed to use a moped on a road once in possession of a provisional driving licence until such time as he has passed an approved training course known as "Compulsory Basic Training" or is undergoing training. A learner must display L plates and cannot carry an unqualified passenger.

If you hold a full car licence you are qualified to ride a moped without L plates. In order to secure a full moped licence, you will have to take a theory test as well as a practical test.

You must be properly supervised by a qualified instructor and wear fluorescent clothing.

You are allowed to ride the moped for a period of two years whilst displaying L plates. To obtain a full licence you must pass a theory test and a further practical test; after passing each stage successfully, you can apply for your full licence.

CATEGORIES OF MOTORCYCLE LICENCE

Type of Motorcycle	Group	Size of Motorcycle
Light motor cycle	A1	75cc-125cc power output 11kw
Standard motor cycle	A	Taken on 120-125cc and capable of 100kph, restricted up to 25kw for two years after which period can ride any speed.

A learner of a large motorcycle must hold a provisional driving licence for the driving of motor bicycles and be at least 21 years of age. Learners must also be under the super-vision of a qualified instructor who can communicate by radio, and the learner must be wearing fluorescent clothing.

If you take a CBT, theory test and take the practical test on a larger motor cycle with an output of at least 35kw, you can ride larger motor cycles before the end of the restricted two year period.

The standard of driving applied to a learner driver is the same as a fully qualified driver, in that the same test is applied, i.e. that of a careful and competent driver.

SUPERVISORS

A supervisor should do what he can be reasonably be expected to do to prevent the learner acting unskilfully or in a manner likely to cause danger. If he fails to do this, he could be guilty of an offence of aiding and abetting an offence.

The following regulations must be followed to be a properly qualified supervisor.

- At least 21 years of age
- Hold a relevant full driving licence for the vehicle being driven
- Relevant driver experience by being a holder of a driving licence for more than three years.
- Must be able to take control of the steering and braking of the vehicle
- Or is a member of the armed forces acting in duty for three years and is over 21 years old.

Payment for supervisory services cannot be taken unless you are a Registered Instructor. As well as the danger of aiding and abetting the learner of motoring offences, a supervisor can commit the following specific motoring offences.

S5(1) Road Traffic Act 1988

Supervising a learner driver with excess alcohol as he is classed as being in charge of the vehicle.

Aiding and abetting a learner driver to drive with excess alcohol.

Driving without insurance

If a supervisor owns the car and is supervising the learner whilst uninsured, he will be guilty of the offence of using a vehicle without insurance. However, if he is supervising in a vehicle not belonging to him, he would be guilty of permitting the use of the vehicle without insurance if he was aware the insurance did not cover the learner driver.

Aiding and abetting offences

There are circumstances when a supervisor may be committing the offence of aiding and abetting an offence by the learner such as careless driving, dangerous driving or mobile phone use.

In order to be found guilty of aiding and abetting, a supervisor must:-

• Know that the standard of driving is below that of a careful competent driver

• Have had the opportunity to stop the learner driver from driving in that manner but failed to do so.

• Have assisted the driver to commit the offence, i.e. by encouraging him to commit the offence or omitting to do something to stop him committing the offence.

NEW DRIVERS

Under the Road Traffic (New Drivers) Act 1995, if a new driver acquires 6 points or more on his licence within two years of passing his test, he may have his licence revoked and be required to resit his test.

The same standard of driving is expected of a new driver, i.e. that of a careful and competent driver.

A new driver may display P plates but there is no legal requirement to do so in England and Wales.

Insurance and New Drivers

There are many issues which can arise with learner drivers and new drivers when it comes to insurance cover. It is often inexpensive to put a learner driver on a current policy, as the learner driver will usually be supervised. However, the difficulty arises when the learner passes and becomes a new driver as premiums shoot through the roof and the temptation is very high to carry on with the policy as it is. This would mean that the new driver is not insured, and as no insurance carries a minimum of 6 points, he would revert back to being a learner driver with fines, costs, and the added costs of re-taking his test etc... As well as that, the parent could also face the charge of permitting no insurance and receive points and a fine. Not informing the insurance company of any change is, in fact, the more expensive option in the long run. If you have misinformed the insurance company, there are also other offences to consider which carry heavier penalties, such as obtaining insurance by deception.

Care should also be taken if part-time work is undertaken which involves the use of the car. The driver must ensure that they have "business use" insurance otherwise they will be classed as using the vehicle without insurance.

Another point to raise with learner drivers and new drivers is that they must comply with the conditions of their licence and the insurance in terms of supervision and displaying plates, etc. Failing to do so may make their insurance void.

Chapter Five
Motorcyclists

MOTORCYCLES

There are a number of regulations which relate to motor-cycles and similar vehicles. I have covered key aspects of these in this chapter.

Types Of Vehicles

A moped
A moped is a motor vehicle which:
- Has an engine capacity not exceeding 50cc
- Does not weigh more than 250kg
- Has a design maximum speed of 50kph (31mph).

A motor bicycle

A motor bicycle is a motor vehicle which:
- Has two wheels
- Has a maximum design speed exceeding 45 kph
- Has a cylinder capacity exceeding 50 cc
- Can include a combination of motor vehicle and side car.

A learner motor bicycle

A leaner motor bicycle is either:
- Propelled by electric power

Or
- The cylinder capacity does not exceed 125 cc
- Maximum power output does not exceed 11kw.

A large motor bicycle

A large motor bicycle is one that
- Has maximum output exceeding 25kw (without sidecar)

OR
- Has a power to weight ratio exceeding 0.16kw per kilogram

OR
- Has a power to weight ratio exceeding 0.16kw per kilogram.

If your motor bicycle is not within this definition or that of a moped/light motorcycle, then it is a standard motorcycle.

Scrambling motorcycles

There is often an issue about the use of scrambling type motorcycles and whether they fall within the definition of a motor vehicle intended or adapted for use on a road.

Generally they are designed solely for use off road, but what is the position – as is often the case – when they are used on the road to get to and from an off road track, or they are used for joy riding in streets and public parks?

If such motorcycles are used on public roads they will be held to be a motor vehicle, as it has been held by the courts that such motorcycles fall within the definition of "adapted for use on a road" by the very fact that they are being ridden for such purposes. This will of course depend on the degree of adaptation and each case will be judged on its merits, but my advice would be that most will be regarded as motor vehicles for the purposes of road traffic legislation, and they should be kept off the road unless they are roadworthy and properly documented with vehicle excise licence, insurance and an MOT. The rider would also be liable for motoring offences relating to motor vehicles i.e. driving without due care and attention.

Go-peds

Go-peds are motorised scooters which are sold with a specific instruction not to use on a road. The argument was that due to this they were not "intended or adapted for use on a road" and therefore did not fall within the definition. However, the court's view was different. If a reasonable person would say that one of the uses would be for use on roads, and use on a road would be contemplated, then it would be a motor vehicle for the purposes of road traffic legislation, thus requiring all the appropriate documentation and the rider being liable for offences relating to a motor vehicle i.e. due care and attention.

A Sidecar

There is no definition for a sidecar but it is classed as part of the motorcycle and not part of its equipment. It must fall within the requirements of Reg 92 of the Road Vehicle (Construction and Use) Regulations 1968 and if it does not, it will be classed as a trailer.

Three-wheeled motor vehicle

If a three-wheeled vehicle does not exceed 410kg it will come within the definition of a motor cycle. Any vehicle over 410kg will be classed a motor car rather than a motor cycle.

Licence Categories

Licence Category	Vehicles you can ride	Requirements for licence	Minimum Age
AM	Mopeds with speed range of 25kph to 45kph	Compulsory basic training (CBT), theory test, practical test on all powered two-wheeled moped	16
AM	Small 3-wheelers (up to 50cc and below 4kw)	CBT, theory test, practical test	16

AM	Light quadricycles (weighing under 350kg, top speed 45kph)	CBT, theory test, practical test	16
Q	Same as AM plus 2 or 3-wheeled mopeds with top speed of 25kph	Granted with AM	16
A1	Light motorcycle up to 11kw (and a power-to-weight ratio not more than 0.11kw per kg) and 125cc	CBT, Theory test, practical test	17
A1	Motor tricycles with a power output not more than 15kw	CBT, Theory test, practical test	17
A2	Standard motorcycle up to 35kw (and a power-to-weight ratio not more than 0.2 kw per kg), bike musn't be derived from vehicle more than twice its power	Direct access rout- theory and practical Staged access route- 2 years' experience on A1 motorbike and a further practical test	19

Insurance

The main issues which relate to motorcycles are those which relate to motor vehicles in general; these are covered in Chapter Three. However, there are certain issues which relate specifically to motorcycles.

Under S148(5) of the Road Traffic Act 1988, certain conditions will be void after the event so in effect, an insurance company cannot attempt to restrict certain conditions; this includes one condition relating to the carriage of passengers. Some motorcycles are designed to carry passengers, whilst others are not. If your motorcycle has a designated seat which is properly secured to the motorcycle, then any attempt to restrict your carriage of passengers other than that imposed by legislation i.e. learners will be unenforceable. So, if involved in an accident, your passenger would be covered and able to claim for any injuries and damage sustained.

If your motorcycle has a side car the same principles would apply, so an insurer would not be able to enforce any condition to restrict the carriage of passengers.

However, if your motorcycle is not designed for a passenger, any restrictions from the insurance company regarding the carriage of a passenger is likely to be valid so your passenger, if involved in an accident, may not be able to claim for personal injury or damage.

Pillion Passengers

Under S23 of the Road Traffic Act 1988, it is an offence to carry more than one passenger on a motorcycle. The penalty is a level 3 fine which is currently £1,000, 3 points or a discretionary disqualification. The passenger must be seated astride a proper seat which is securely behind the driver's seat.

Motorcycle Crash Helmet and Eye Protectors

Motorcycle Crash Helmet

Anyone riding or driving a motorcycle must wear protective headgear which complies with the requirements of Regulation 4 of the Motor Cycles (Protective Helmets) Regulations 1998. The head gear must be securely fastened by straps and must bear an approved quality standard mark. It is an offence not to comply with these requirements; the penalty is a level 2 fine, currently £500.

There are exceptions when using a mowing machine and if you are a member of the Sikh religion wearing a turban.

The sale of non-prescribed helmets is also an offence, carrying a level 3 fine of £1,000.

Eye Protectors

A motorcyclist does not have to wear eye protection but if you choose to, they must comply with the Motor Cycle (Eye Protection) Regulations 1999. These provide the minimum standards of compliance. It is an offence to use non-compliant eye protection; the penalty is a level 2 fine of £500. It is also an offence to sell non-compliant eye protection, the penalty is a level 3 fine of £1,000.

Chapter Six
Notice of Intended Prosecution and Driver Information Requests

For certain offences, the police must give a notice of their intended prosecution. These are listed in Schedule 1 of the Road Traffic Offenders Act 1988 and are as follows:-

Legislation	Offence
S2 ROAD TRAFFIC ACT 1998 (RTA 1988)	Dangerous driving
S3 RTA 1988	Careless and inconsiderate driving
S22 RTA 1988	Leaving a vehicle in a dangerous position
S28 RTA 1988	Dangerous Cycling
S29 RTA 1988	Careless and inconsiderate Cycling

S35 RTA 1988	Failure to comply with a traffic direction
S36 RTA 1988	Failure to comply with traffic signs
S88(7) and S89(1) RTA 1988	Speeding including motorways
S14 and S16 Road Traffic Regulation Act 1984 (RTRA 1984)	Temporary Speeding restrictions

Aiding and abetting all the above offences also require a notice of intended prosecution.

The purpose is to give the driver of the vehicle some notice that a prosecution is intended so that evidence can be retained and put forward by the defence. As the police in most road traffic cases have a time limit of 6 months to summons, many cases are issued very close to the deadline, and as such the notice assures that a defendant is not taken by surprise by a summons for motoring offences and either cannot remember or has lost evidence as a result of any delay.

NOTE

The requirement for a notice does not apply to:-

• Any offences other than those listed above, even if the offence itself is similar in nature.

• Offences of dangerous driving, careless driving, inconsiderate driving if at the time of the offence or immediately after a road traffic accident occurs, on the basis that if there was an accident, the driver would be aware.

• Offences where a fixed penalty notice has been given.

NOTICE OF INTENDED PROSECUTION

A notice of prosecution must:
- Be served on the driver/registered keeper
- Be served within 14 days of the alleged incident
- Be sent by registered/recorded or First Class post on last known address or
- Personal service

If the identity of the driver is not known, then the police will issue a notice to the registered keeper, the details of whom they can get from the registration number via the DVLA. If this is not the actual driver it will not invalidate the notice if the driver gets a notice outside the 14 day period, as long as the notice sent to the registered keeper is within the 14 day period.

The notice can be given orally with words to the effect of "You will be reported for consideration of the question of prosecuting you for (offence/s)". If you are issued with a HORT/1 requiring production of driving documents, this is written on the form and will be signed by the officer.

There is a presumption that the notice has been properly served in time, so you must put the prosecution on notice if you are to take issue with this. It is often a good idea to raise it with the police prior to issuing the summons, as the effect of failing to comply with the time period is usually fatal to the case. However, the police can claim that they acted with reasonable diligence in attempting to locate the person on whom the notice should be served i.e. the registered keeper or the driver. In most cases, if the vehicle registration number is taken, this will not be difficult, so the police will not succeed if this is the case. Consider, however, if only a part registration has been taken, or no registration, this would delay the issuing of any notice and as long as the police did everything in their power as quickly as reasonably possible then they would have an argument. Once they have received the relevant information, the 14 day limit would certainly be enforced and if outside this period any argument for reasonable diligence is likely to fail.

Where a notice is sent by registered or recorded delivery but is returned to the sender, service is still valid for the purposes of this legislation. First class post-delivery is classed as served unless and until the contrary is proved. It imperative, therefore, that if you receive a notice of intended prosecution, you date stamp the envelope and the letter if you received it out of time by first class post.

Errors on the Notice of Intended Prosecution

Errors on the notice of intended prosecution are not usually fatal to the case as long as the notice still has the desired effect i.e. notifying someone about a prosecution.

There would be issues if the driver could not identify the incident at all; perhaps because it is too vague, or relates to a different incident than the one he remembers being involved with. This is when it gets a little complicated, and you would have to consider the facts against previous case law to establish whether or not it was fatal.

This area of law is a minefield, as notices can be served in different ways, within differing periods and contain various errors. It is advisable to contact a road traffic expert such as Auriga Advocates who can give you initial free advice with a clear indication as to whether or not you have a challenge based on the Notice of Intended Prosecution. They can then, for a fixed fee, challenge the NIP for you.

Request For Driver Information/ S172 Notice

If you have not been stopped at the time of the offence then you will receive an NIP as previously discussed; because the driver ID will not be known, it should also contain an S172 Notice, which is a form requesting the details of the driver.

It is not the NIP and does not have the same requirements, so even if it is received outside the 14 day deadline for the NIP this should still be completed and returned because it is an offence not to do so.

The offence is usually dealt with by way of a penalty of a £600 fine and 6 points, but the fine maximum is £1,000 so is usually more severe than the penalty for the offence. If you are in doubt contact a road traffic specialist who can give you some guidance on whether you should complete it, who should complete it and with what details. Any person addressed on the S172 has the obligation to comply with the request, which usually requires a signature. To fulfil the requirement, all details should be provided and if required it should be signed.

If you receive an S172 in your name, it is imperative that you complete the form and sign it. Nobody else should do this on your behalf, not even if they are the driver. Once named, the driver will receive an S172 notice in his name to confirm the position. You must NEVER complete the form with false details, as this is a much more serious offence which carries imprisonment.

It is a defence if you:-
• Do not know the driver
AND
• Could not have ascertained with reasonable diligence who the driver of the vehicle was.

It is not an easy defence to argue, because if you own a car you should always obtain details of who the driver is before you allow them to drive your car. If you do not and you receive a S172 notice, it will not be a defence to say, "I did not know the driver's name," because the defence requires "reasonable diligence" and allowing someone to drive your car without ascertaining who they are is not reasonable diligence.

If you have not received the notice and the summons has been issued, it will be too late to supply the information. If there is good reason for not receiving the S172 notice, such as postal issues, you may have a defence because it was not reasonably practical to respond within the 28 days, because you had not received the S172 notice. You cannot reasonably respond to something you have never received.

However, if you have not received the notice because you have moved house and not informed the DVLA, this defence will not work because you will have brought it on yourself. You should note also that failing to notify the DVLA of a change of address is also an offence.

Companies

Companies are classed as a separate legal person so if the registered keeper is a limited company, the NIP and the S172 will be served on the company, normally to the company secretary at the registered office. The individual person in the company responsible for responding will also be liable for the offence, so they would risk an endorsement of 6 points if it is shown that it has been committed with the consent or connivance of, or to be attributable to neglect on the part of, a director, manager, secretary or other similar office of the company.

This prevents directors from ignoring an S172 so that the

company alone gets a fine and no-one gets points on their licence, which used to be the case. It also means that a director cannot say he does not know who the driver was, because unless he can demonstrate that the company has clear policies and procedures for identifying who is driving a particular company car, the director will be liable.

The S172 notice must be completed by the person to whom the notice is written, despite the fact that it may be some other person's role within the company.

Chapter Seven
Speeding

Speeding is endemic in Britain and is seen as socially acceptable; most of us at some time will be prosecuted for speeding or required to attend a speeding awareness course.

There is a clear proven causal link between speeding and fatal/serious injury accidents and it is well documented that if hit at the speed of 40mph, you are more than four times more likely to suffer death than if hit at the speed of 30mph. In 2013, 3064 people were killed or seriously injured in the UK from speeding incidents so it is not surprising, therefore, that the regulation of speeding is a high priority.

Motorists often feel persecuted by speeding limits, police detection and roadside cameras and the government is aware of this; recent guidelines have been produced in an attempt to redress the balance.

Joining Forces for Safer Roads

"The road policing ethos is to deliver a crucial protective service that engenders public satisfaction and service."

The aims of the guidelines are to secure safer roads through:-

- Maximum compliance
- Education in preference to punishment
- Enforcement of habitual or serious offenders

The higher mileage that a motorist drives is likely to put that driver at a greater risk of falling foul of the speeding legislation, so this chapter could prove invaluable.

TYPES OF ROADS

There are two types of road:-

- Restricted
- De-restricted

Restricted Roads

Restricted roads are subject to a speed limit of 30mph under S81 Road Traffic Regulation Act 1984. The characteristics of a restricted road are governed by S82 of the Road Traffic Regulation Act 1984, which are:-

- Road lamps placed not more than 200 yards apart (not a built-up area which is a motorist's myth)
- No requirement for speed limit signs

- Road with this lamp system will be restricted unless otherwise indicated.

This means that a motorist should be aware when a road is restricted, because there is no defence available that there were no signs if a lighting system is in place. It will not be a defence that some lamps were more than 200 yards apart, particularly if it is only odd lamps which are further apart. However, it could be a defence if the system were to be totally lacking in any lamp system it is all a question of degree. If the lighting system appears to be totally lacking, your best defence is to take photographs and get your measuring tape out. Once armed with your evidence, discuss the issue with a specialist lawyer who, with reference to the mass of case law around this area, will be able to advise you accordingly.

You should also be aware that a local authority can restrict a road without a lighting system, but the road would then have to be signposted in accordance with S85 of the Road Traffic Regulation Act 1984 and the Traffic Signs Regulations & General Directions 2002/2013.

If you receive a summons it is also worth checking that the section you are summonsed under is the correct one i.e. in the case of restricted road it would be contrary to S81. But be warned, this in itself will not be a defence because the prosecution, if warned about or having realised the mistake, can amend the summons after the close of the defence case, which weakens the defence argument. It is only if the defendant is prejudiced that such amendment will not be allowed, so if the defendant knew the charge he was facing then he will not be deemed to be prejudiced.

Generally, therefore, it will be difficult to defend a restricted road speeding matter unless there are some serious deficiencies in the lamp system.

However, the position is different for de-restricted roads.

De-Restricted Roads

De-restricted roads are those without a lamp system, and no motorist can be convicted of a speeding offence unless the speed is limited by the presence of properly place speed limit signs.

There are regulations in relation to the size of signs and the position of them. You can find full details on the Traffic Signs Regulations & General Directions 2002/2013 which you can download from the internet. You can also refer to the Department for Transport Traffic Signs Manual.

Signs must be at the beginning and the end of the section of road to which the speed limit applies.

Figure 14-1
Terminal signs for single carriageway road

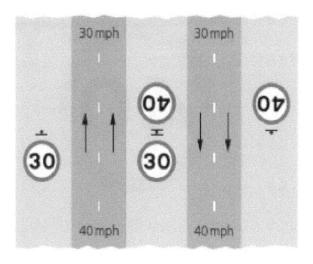

Figure 14-2
Terminal signs for dual carriageway road

On wide central reservations the two signs should be mounted separately, closer to each carriageway

Repeater signs must be placed at regular intervals along the road between the starter and terminating signs and should be 300mm in diameter. Signs MUST be illuminated during the hours of darkness.

They must also comply with the regulations in terms of their form, i.e. size of signs and numbering.

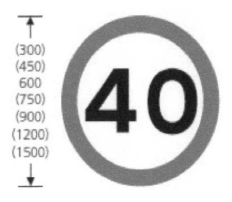

670 Maximum speed limit in miles per hour

The numerals may be varied (see para 14.4)

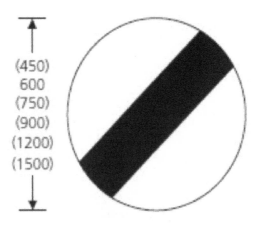

671 National speed limits apply

Repeater signs should be 300mm in diameter. Note that signs with a red border are mandatory, whereas signs with a black border are advisory; but exceeding these could still result in a prosecution for offences other than speeding, such as driving without due care and attention or inconsiderate driving. Remember, a de-restricted road must have lawfully sized and postioned signage to enforce the speed limit as no conviction can be made without it. The regulations change frequently, and often councils do not keep up with updating road signs, so it is often only new roads which comply with the latest regulations. Older signs are often worn or broken, which can affect their legal impact.

It is debatable whether the fact that signs are covered with foliage or otherwise not visible means they are in breach of the regulations, as the regulations only regulate format and position. Passing comments in judgements of cases dealing with de-restricted roads suggest that such signs would not be in breach of the regulations for that very reason, but that seems an illogical argument to me. I would be inclined to suggest that visiblity is implied by the regulations, because the regulations are so prescriptive in terms of size and position that the only purpose of them is to ensure that the motorist is aware of the speed limit and can see them. We will have to await case law or legislation for the definitive answer.

Don't forget that the "de minimis rule" will apply to these signs as well, so if only one repeater sign was not visible, it is likely that the court would still hold the signage as lawful, so any breaches in the regulations would need to be quite significant.

Cotterill V Chapman 1984

"In all these cases of men painting signs on a road, or, using those machines with whitened rollers with which we are so familiar, a moment's pause for reflections will show that it is inevitable that from time to time there will be trivial departures from any prescribed minimum or maximum. To hold in such circumstances that any departure, however trivial, renders a motorist immune from prosecution if he disregards a sign will virtually render this part of our road traffic law a nullity."

SPEED LIMITS

Temporary Speed Limits

Unless the speed limit is signed to the contrary the following applies:-

- Unrestricted dual carriageway is limited to 70 mph
- Unrestricted single carriageway is limited to 60 mph

Roads with the national limit of 70mph or 60 mph do not require speed limit signs, but those limited to 50mph, whether single/dual carriageway, or 60mph on a dual carriageway do. Signs must be displayed if there is any temporary restrictions due to roadworks; these cannot be in force for longer than 18 months and signs must be displayed.

Motorway Speed Limits

Motorways have a speed limit of 70mph, but if there are any reduced speed limits there must be signs displayed as in accordance with any other road. The signs are 1200mm and can be placed on gantries.

Vehicle Speed Limits

Certain classes of vehicle are limited to different speeds; please see the table below.

Class of Vehicle	Motor-way	Dual C/way	Other Road
A passenger vehicle, motor caravan or dual-purpose vehicle not drawing a trailer being a vehicle with an unladen weight exceeding 3.05 tonnes or adapted to carry more than 8 passengers:			
(i) if not exceeding 12 metres in overall length	70	60	50
(ii) if exceeding 12 metres in overall length	60	60	50

An invalid carriage	N/A	20	20
A passenger vehicle, motor caravan, car-derived van or dual-purpose vehicle drawing one trailer	60	60	50
A passenger vehicle, motor caravan, car-derived van or dual-purpose vehicle drawing more than one trailer	40	20	20
(1) A goods vehicle having a maximum laden weight not exceeding 7.5 tonnes and which is not—			
(a) an articulated vehicle, or	70	60	50

(b) drawing a trailer, or (c) a car-derived van (2) A goods vehicle which is— a) (i) an articulated vehicle having a maximum laden weight not exceeding 7.5 tonnes, or (ii) a motor vehicle, other than a car-derived van, which is drawing one trailer where the aggregate maximum laden weight of the motor vehicle and the trailer does not exceed 7.5 tonnes	60	60	50

(b) (i) an articulated vehicle having a maximum laden weight exceeding 7.5 tonnes,			
(ii) a motor vehicle having a maximum laden weight exceeding 7.5 tonnes and not drawing a trailer,	60	60	50
or			
(iii) a motor vehicle drawing one trailer where the aggregate maximum laden weight of the motor vehicle and the trailer exceeds 7.5 tonnes	40	20	20

c) a motor vehicle, other than a car-derived van, drawing more than one trailer	40	20	20
A motor tractor (other than an industrial tractor), a light locomotive or a heavy locomotive—			
(a) if the provisions about springs and wings as specified in paragraph 3 of Part IV of this Schedule are complied with and the vehicle is not drawing a trailer, or if those provisions are complied with and the vehicle is drawing one trailer which also complies with those provisions	40	30	30
b) in any other case	20	20	20

A works truck	18	18	18
An industrial tractor	N/A	18	18
An Agricultural Motor Vehicle	40	40	40

SPEED CHECK METHODS

There are a number of methods which the police use to check a motorist's speed. If the police use any device to measure the speed, that device must be approved and used in accordance with operating manuals which are readily available online. ACPO guidelines provide the police with guidance as to how and when devices should be used. These devices are used to corroborate an officer's opinion that a vehicle is speeding, and he must demonstrate that he held this opinion, as opposed to just targeting every vehicle. The prosecution must serve the evidence from the device on you at least 7 days before the trial, and you have three days before the trial to request the attendance of the officer using the device. This may be required if you are disputing whether the device was used properly. If they fail to serve the evidence, the prosecution cannot prove their case, but it is a gamble because if they do, you will still need to defend your case and should be prepared with further evidence suggested below. If that is all you are relying on, if the evidence is served you may be forced to plead guilty. However, the police do not usually serve such evidence with the summons and often not even when requested. Therefore, in most cases the evidence will not be served until there is a not guilty plea. This means that the police must send the evidence to the CPS; in recent experience, both are under pressure and road traffic offences are lower priority than substantive crime so they are not reviewed in the same way. Often prosecutors only pick the case up the day before trial or on the day of trial, so often the vital evidence is either not on the file at all, or is but has not been served.

There are a number of points to check if stopped by any device:-

• Is the device approved (S20 Road Traffic Offenders Act 1988)
• Has the device been operated by a properly trained officer?
• Has the officer followed the operator's manual?
• Visit http://bcove.me/jr337i34 for examples of officers' operating devices.

The point to remember with any device, whether operated by an officer or a fixed device: we have not reached the stage in evidence where machine evidence is conclusive, as machines can, and do, go wrong.

Kent V Stamps 1963 Rtr 273

"The basic principle must be that the reading on the machine is evidence. It is very cogent evidence indeed, and in the vast majority of cases one would suppose that it was conclusive evidence. But we have not reached the stage when the reading on such a piece of apparatus as this has to be accepted as absolutely accurate and true, no matter what. There are all kinds of things in a case like this which might have gone wrong."

There are several types of device, of which the main ones are as follows:-

- Fixed Camera – Gatso/Truvelo
- Laser
- Radar
- Vascar

Fixed Camera

These are the fixed roadside cameras, which are mainly GATSO cameras. These are rear facing cameras so do not obtain a photograph of the driver. There are usually white lines on the road which offer a second measurement of speed. These are a set distance apart, usually 5ft, and reflect 5mph, so that your speed can be checked against that of the reading provided by the device. These are limited in use to zones 30mph and above.

If you wish to check this, you will need a copy of the photograph, which some forces will not disclose until such time as you have pleaded not guilty, thus increasing your costs. However, there are strong arguments to keep costs down, because you had not been disclosed with all the relevant material in order to determine your guilt or otherwise.

Once you have your photograph, you should be able to make the appropriate calculations which are as follows:-

Gap x *distance between lines/marks* (usually 5ft) / 0.5(the usual time lapse between photographs) x 0.6818 = SPEED

The GATSO can record the speed limit relevant to different types of vehicles, but due to the use of film, once the film is used it will not record any further speeding offences which will occur in very busy areas. One key point to remember is that although they do not have a picture of the driver, any Notice of Intended Prosecution (NIP) will be sent to the registered keeper with an S172 notice, which is a form requiring the identification of the driver. It is an offence not to identify the driver, and providing the wrong details is more serious.

In some areas they use a fixed camera called a Truvelo which takes a photograph of the front of the vehicle.

It uses piezo sensors in the road at a certain distance apart; as a vehicle goes over the sensors, the device measures the speed and triggers the camera if over the limit (D Cam P) or a laser which can measure the speed of approaching vehicles (D Cam L). These do not flash, so lack of a flash is no indication that you have not been recorded for speeding. Also, because they are digital, they can store far more images and these can be downloaded in real time to the police prosecutions department. These are used in Hampshire and Northamptonshire, and many areas are changing from GATSO to Truvelo over time.

It is important to note that as these take front pictures, you must ensure that you complete the S172 accurately because the photograph may show that any falsely named driver could not have been the person driving. This is an offence of perverting the course of justice, and carries heavy penalties of imprisonment.

Laser

Laser devices are very accurate when used properly, however the following points should be considered:-

• The police officer must be trained in using that particular laser device
• The laser gun must be calibrated in accordance with the manual
• The police officer must be using it within the manual's instructions
• It must be aimed accurately at the target vehicle
• It must not be used through a windscreen
• It can only be used when the target vehicle is travelling in a straight line.

If you are intending to defend a case involving such a device, you must inform the prosecution that you want evidence of the approval and that you are taking issue with the device or use thereof. There is a presumption that the device is functioning properly, so it is vital if you wish to defend your case that evidence is introduced. The only way you can do this is to put the prosecution to proof on the point, so that they have to produce evidence.

You can also get evidence about the manual, usually online or from the manufacturer, but care must be taken that the manual you are referring to does relate to the device used.

You may also benefit with your defence by reference to the ACPO guidelines, which produce guidance on the use of laser devices, but note: "The manufacturers' instructions therefore form the most relevant operating procedures to be carried out when operating each piece of equipment. This guide explains the reasoning behind some of the instructions in operator manuals but is subservient to them. The advice in this guide should be used to enhance the operators' manual."

ACPO guide for the operational use of speed and red-light offence detection technology

You will get evidence excluded by the fact that an officer has failed to use the device properly, but you will bring into question the accuracy of the speed. As a defendant you only have to cast doubt on the prosecution evidence and it is the prosecution's role to prove the case beyond all reasonable doubt, so evidence of non-compliance can result in an acquittal.

Radar

Radar devices should be approved and calibrated at least once a year by the manufacturer. They work on what is known as the "Doppler effect", whereby the gun is pointed at a moving vehicle. A radar beam is sent to the vehicle which, once struck, reflects the beam back to the gun. The frequency at which the beam is reflected back is proportionate to the speed of the vehicle.

There are a number of ways in which these guns can give a false reading:-

- Low batteries
- Poor connection through car lighter sockets
- Radio interference
- Other objects/vehicles interfere so you cannot be sure which has been read

• A test on a small vehicle can pick up a larger vehicle behind.

The officer should check the radar gun against the speedometer of the police vehicle before and after use.

The police vehicle's speedometer should also have been calibrated on an annual basis. When using the device, an officer must ensure that he selects a position with a clear view of the road.

Once the device is pointed at the vehicle and a reading taken, he should observe the reading for at least three seconds to ensure the reading stays steady. If it is not, the reading is erroneous and should be discarded.

Courts are more inclined to find that radar readings are inaccurate because there are so many factors which influence the reading.

You should insist on all the evidence:-

• Calibration of the radar gun and the police vehicle
• Exact location of the device on the road with a map
• Any CCTV at the location
• Qualifications of the police officer to use the device

Once received, you should check the evidence carefully and ask further questions if necessary, such as their position from radio activity, whether the officer had his mobile phone on and what other traffic was about. You should have made notes at the time of any other vehicles about, particularly anything close to your vehicle which could have impacted on the radar beam.

A specialist solicitor could always do this for you if you are unsure as to what to do.

Vascar

Vascar is a device which is manually operated by a police officer in a police vehicle. It basically measures the distance between two points, and from the time it has taken to get from point A to point B, it calculates the average speed. It is reasonably accurate but relies heavily on the officer's accuracy at triggering the device at the points observed, so such officers need to be trained and evidence of their qualification to use the device should be insisted upon. This does need to be calibrated, and evidence of this should also be requested.

APPENDIX 5 Sentencing guidelines for Speeding.

Chapter Eight
Dangerous, Careless and Inconsiderate Driving

DANGEROUS DRIVING OFFENCES

There are three offences in the dangerous driving category, these are:-

1. Causing death by dangerous driving
2. Causing serious injury by dangerous driving
3. Dangerous driving

Causing Death By Dangerous Driving

It is an offence to cause the death of another person by driving a mechanically propelled vehicle dangerously on a road or public place. The penalty is a maximum of 14 years imprisonment, a minimum disqualification of two years with extended re-test.

This offence differs from other offences such as document offences because it relates to mechanically propelled vehicles (MPV), not just a motor vehicle; therefore, even vehicles not intended for use or adapted for use on a road will qualify under the definition. It includes public places as well as roads, e.g. car parks.

It is an indictable-only offence which means that it will be sent directly to the Crown Court. In light of the serious nature of this offence, I would not advise anyone to represent themselves. If you are arrested on suspicion of such an offence, you should seek legal advice immediately.

Causing Serious Injury By Dangerous Driving

It is an offence to cause serious injury whilst driving an MPV dangerously on a road or public place. This offence was introduced in December 2012 to offer the courts an interim sentencing range between dangerous driving and death by dangerous driving.

The same principles apply as to death by dangerous driving in relation to the type of vehicle, road and public place. The penalty is up to 5 years imprisonment/unlimited fine and a disqualification of a minimum of two years and extended re-test.

This is an either way offence, which can be dealt with in the Magistrates Court or the Crown Court.

If dealt with in the Magistrates Court, the offence will be maximum of 6 months imprisonment/level 5 fine, currently at £5,000/unlimited from the 12th March 2015. The same disqualification applies.

I would advise you to seek immediate specialist advice if you are being investigated or have been charged with this offence.

Note that you may avoid a compulsory disqualification if you are able to establish that special reasons apply for non-disqualification. (Chapter 13)

Dangerous Driving

It is an offence to drive an MPV dangerously on a road or other public place. The penalty is a maximum of two years imprisonment with a disqualification of at least a year and extended re-test, unless special reasons are applicable.

This is an either way offence which can be dealt with in the Magistrates Court or the Crown Court.

The definition of dangerous driving is:-

• The standard of driving falls far below what would be expected of a competent and careful driver;
   AND
• It would be obvious to a competent and careful driver that driving in that way would be dangerous.

The test is an objective test, so it does not matter what the driver appreciated, but what an average driver would think was dangerous according to the test. It is really a matter of judgement, and each case rests on its merits. For example, running a red light at a busy junction would probably be considered dangerous; but what if, when running the red light, the junction was clear because it was the early hours of the morning – would the decision be the same? Probably not.

These offences are serious and much rests on this definition and the interpretation and application of the facts. There are numerous evidential issues which can arise in such cases, even with a trial at the Magistrates Court, so expert advice is always recommended.

NOTE: An NIP is required for this offence if there is no accident (See Chapter 6).

Appendix 6 Sentencing guidelines for dangerous driving

CARELESS AND INCONSIDERATE DRIVING

There are three offences within this category as follows:-

1. Death by careless and inconsiderate driving
2. Driving without due care and attention (careless driving)
3. Driving without reasonable consideration.

Death By Careless And Inconsiderate Driving

This is a similar offence to that of causing death by dangerous driving, but less serious, with a lower test for the standard of driving. It is an offence to cause a death by driving an MPV without due care and attention, or without reasonable consideration on a road or public place. The penalty is a maximum of 5 years/unlimited fine, a disqualification of 12 months and discretionary extended re-test.

Appendix 7 Sentencing guidelines for death by careless or inconsiderate driving

Driving Without Due Care And Attention (Careless Driving)

It is an offence to drive without due care and attention. The penalty is level 5 fine, currently £5,000/unlimited for offences committed after the 12th March 2015, discretionary disqualification or a mandatory endorsement of 3-9 points.

NOTE: An NIP is required for this offence if there is no accident (See chapter 6).

The definition of driving without due care and attention is:-

• That the standard of driving fell below that of a reasonable competent and careful driver.

Even if you did not know about the accident you could still be liable, although you would not be guilty of failing to stop or report the accident. (see Chapter 9)

The test is an objective one, and usually the Magistrates will apply their own views as to what falls below the standard required.

Examples could be:-

• falling asleep at the wheel
• driving with a known mechanical defect
• driving with poor visibility, indicating one way then turning another.

It is a question of judgement and each case will rest on its merits. The standard is the same for every driver and it is not adjusted based on experience of the driver, i.e. whether a learner, new driver or advanced police driver, the test will be applied equally.

Sometimes the facts speak for themselves (Res ipsa loquiter) and you could be prosecuted due to the consequences of your driving, such as mounting a pavement and hitting a lamppost. If this is the case, then the prosecution can use the presumption that you have driven without due care and attention because in the normal course of events, if driving carefully you would not have had the accident – i.e. the facts speak for themselves. Of course, this is only a presumption and can be rebutted, so for example, you may have swerved to avoid a child who ran into the road or had an unforeseen mechanical defect.

Driving Without Reasonable Consideration

It is an offence to drive an MPV without reasonable consideration for others. It must be shown that you have inconvenienced the other person; examples would be driving through a puddle, wetting the pedestrians close by.

The penalties are the same as for driving without due care and attention. This is a more unusual offence than driving without due care and attention, but is often used for driving which is regarded as thoughtless, rather than without due care. Examples would be going too slow on the motorway or hogging the middle lane.

Appendix 8 Sentencing guidelines on careless or inconsiderate driving

NOTE: An NIP is required for this offence if there is no accident (see Chapter 6). Either offence can be dealt with by way of a fixed penalty notice (see Chapter 2) OR a Driver Improvement Course (see Chapter 1).

Chapter Nine
Failing to Stop and
Report

If an accident has occurred, which involves a mechanically propelled vehicle (including off road vehicles), whether the driver of that vehicle caused the accident or not, and it results in personal injury or damage to property, then there is a duty for the drivers to stop and provide details to anyone with reasonable grounds to request information.

"Property" includes any vehicle except that of the driver causing the accident. Vehicle could include bicycles, prams, pushchairs and scooters. Property can be attached to land, such as fences, walls or lampposts, and animals. Animals include horses, cattle, asses, mules, sheep, pigs, goats or dogs, but not cats.

The offence is as follows:-

The driver of a mechanically propelled vehicle must stop AND if required to do so by any person having reasonable grounds for so requiring give his name and address and also the name and address of the owner and registration mark of the vehicle. (S170(1) and (2) Road Traffic Act 1988).

The penalty for failing to comply is 6 month imprisonment/level 5 fine, currently £5,000/unlimited fine for offences committed after the 12th March 2015, 5-10 penalty points or discretionary disqualification.

It is also an offence under S168 of the Road Traffic Act 1988 for a driver or cyclist alleged to have committed an offence of dangerous or careless driving or cycling to refuse to give another person his name and address or to provide false details. There does not have to have been an accident under this provision.

The penalty is the same as failing to stop and report. Note also under S154 of the Road Traffic Act 1988 it is a requirement to disclose whether you are insured, provide details and if not insured you are still have a requirement to inform the third party as such.

"Stop" means to stop and remain at the scene of the accident for as long as is reasonable under the circumstances to enable anyone who would have the right to the information time to make the enquiry. It is not a duty on the driver to make enquiries such as knocking on houses etc. (Mutton v Bates (No.1) 1984). The duty is to stop at the scene and not a few yards down the road, but it is unlikely that someone would be prosecuted if they stopped a short distance from the scene, within sight of others involved, in order to exchange details safely.

The issue would arise when no-one has seen you leave and therefore cannot make the request for the details.

The driver must have "knowledge" of the accident. You will not successfully avoid this duty by stating that you heard and felt nothing despite the fact you have obvious damage to your vehicle. You must remember that the Magistrates judging you are likely to be drivers themselves, who will know from their own experience the type of impact which will be felt or heard in a car. It is likely that lack of knowledge is only likely to succeed where the damage is minimal. The test is whether the driver knew of the accident or would have been aware of the accident. The onus to prove lack of knowledge is on the defendant, as there is a presumption that if you are involved in an accident, you will be aware of it. If you intend to defend your case with this argument, you should seek advice from a specialist solicitor. Most specialists, such as Auriga Advocates, will give some free legal advice.

DUTY TO REPORT

Under S170 there is also a duty to report the accident if you have been unable to exchange details at the scene. The duty to report will still apply if you have had the opportunity to exchange details, but have not done so. It will also still apply if there has been personal injury, as there is a duty to provide insurance details under S170(5) and if not provided at the scene, the duty to report it still remains.

It will not suffice to wait for the police to take action, because even if they do so within 24 hours, you will still be guilty of failing to report as soon as reasonably practicable. The penalty for failing to report is the same as failing to stop.

Sometimes when you try to report an accident the police control room will say you don't need to, but unless you have exchanged all relevant information, including insurance, where there is personal injury then you must insist that the details are taken. If not, you must make a note of the call in full including the date, time, number called, name of the operator etc. as well as what was said. If you can record the call, all the better.

It is important to realise that with both these offences it does not matter whether you were at fault; the requirement is for a driver of a mechanically propelled vehicle "involved" in an accident. It does not specify "caused".

This area of road traffic legislation is one worth learning

so that if, unfortunately, you are in an accident, you do not panic or react in a way that will be detrimental to you. The chances are that if you are involved in an accident someone will have noted your registration, so the police will be able to trace you. If you fail to stop or report, it is highly likely the penalty will be higher than the offence which led to the incident. In fact, very often if details are exchanged in full at the scene, the involvement of the police can be avoided altogether.

It is useful to get the business card of a specialist company such as Auriga Advocates to keep with you, as you will be able to call for immediate advice. This advice will be free from most firms.

Appendix 9 Sentencing guidelines to failing to stop/ report

Chapter Ten
Using a Mobile Phone Whilst Driving and Not Being In Proper Control

USING A MOBILE PHONE WHILST DRIVING

The law in relation to mobiles was enacted due to the considerable evidence that mobile use whilst driving led to fatal accidents due to the distraction that it caused to the driver.

Under S41D of the Road Traffic Act 1988 and the Road Vehicle (Construction and Use) Regulations 1986 Reg 110, it is an offence to:-

Drive a vehicle (includes motorcycles) on a road OR to cause or permit any person to drive a vehicle whilst using

- Hand-held mobile phone
- Hand-held device (a device which is not a two-way radio which performs an interactive communication function by transmitting and receiving data)

OR

Causing or permitting any person to drive a vehicle whilst using a hand-held mobile phone or device.

It is also an offence for the supervisor to use a hand-held device under the same circumstances. Note that if the provisional driver is using the mobile phone, the supervisor could be guilty of aiding and abetting the offence under S41D.

Hand-held

A device will be hand-held if it is or must be held at some point during the course of making or receiving a call or performing any other interactive communication function. This will include texting, calling, internet access, faxing, and Instagram inter alia.

If it is held at any point, even if only to connect the call for a moment, the offence is committed.

If you use the mobile phone whilst it is attached to the dashboard, care should be taken as you may fall foul of S41D (a) of the Road Traffic Act 1988 – not being in proper control of a motor vehicle, which carries the same penalty.

You may remember the case of Jimmy Carr at Harrow

Magistrates Court 2009 where he was acquitted of the offence of using a mobile phone. In his defence, he claimed that he was using his mobile phone as a dictaphone to record a joke and therefore was not using a device under the legislation, because he was not using it as an interactive communication. A case in the Magistrates Court does not create a precedent, so other courts are not bound to follow the decision. Another bench may not come to the same conclusion, so before running this defence you are best advised to seek legal advice and representation.

Defence

It is a defence to use a mobile phone under these circumstances:-

• In an emergency to call 112 or 999.
• In genuine emergency and it is unsafe or impracticable to stop to make a call.
• You are not driving but safely parked. Stopping in a line of traffic or at a traffic will still be considered to be driving to ensure you can established you are parked safely you should have pulled over to the kerb, stopped and turned engine off.

The offence will usually be dealt with by way of a Fixed Penalty Notice with 6 points and £200 for offences committed after 1 March 2017. If summonsed to court it carries a penalty of a level 4 fine of £2,500 if carrying more than 8 passengers, and 6 points. For all others it carries a level 3 fine of £1,000 and 6 points.

FAILING TO HAVE PROPER CONTROL

It is an offence to "be in such a position that you cannot have proper control of the vehicle OR full view of the road ahead" according to S41D (a) of the Road Traffic Act 1988.

This could include actions such as:-

- drinking
- eating
- reading newspapers or maps
- putting make-up on
- using a phone for something other than a call/text (as this would be charged   under S41D(b)).

There are few precedents under this section to date, and therefore little guidance. Many drivers are accepting the penalty notice without challenging it, although they feel the penalty is unjustified. Many motorists have informed me that the officer stopping them has informed them that it is an offence to drink or eat whilst driving, which strictly speaking is not true. My view is that if the government wished to make drinking, eating and such like whilst driving an offence, wording specifying that would have been created; it was not. It is a question of degree and there should be some evidence that there is a lack of control such as weaving or not observing the traffic/pedestrians in so me way. Mo re of these cases should be defended to establish clear guidance as to what constitutes this offence, as many drivers are being unjustly penalised at present. Advice should be sought before defending this offence; remember many specialist firms will give free advice.

The penalty if dealt with by way of a fixed penalty ticket is £100 and 3 points. If summonsed the penalty will be a level 3 fine of £1000 max or level 4 fine of £2500 max if carrying more than 8 passengers and 3 points.

Chapter Eleven
Drink Driving and
Related Offences

There are a number of offences which relate to driving whilst under the influence of alcohol or drugs.

These are:-

- Failing to provide a roadside breath test
- Failing to provide a specimen at the police station/hospital
- Driving/attempting to drive with excess alcohol/drugs
- Being in charge of a vehicle with excess alcohol/drugs

PRELIMINARY TESTS

Alcohol

Most of us will probably be stopped by a police officer whilst driving our car because we caught his attention due to poor driving, or a fault on the car such as faulty light. A police officer cannot stop you just to administer a test, but he can stop you randomly. Once stopped, if he reasonably suspects that you are under the influence of a substance, whether that be alcohol or drugs, he can request that you provide a preliminary test. The officer must be in uniform so that it is clear he is a police officer. An officer can also request a test from any person believes to be involved in an accident.

If you have gone into private property, the police have no power of entry to request the preliminary breath test or arrest, except where the officer reasonably suspects that there has been an accident in which injury was caused to any person. However, whilst this should prevent a conviction for failing to provide the preliminary test, it will have no impact at all on the substantive offence of driving with excess alcohol or drugs.

The alcohol test is a roadside breath test which gives the officer an indication of the alcohol level. It is not sufficiently accurate to base a prosecution on, which is why a further test is required if the first test is positive. It is an offence to fail to provide a roadside breath test which carries a penalty of a level 3 fine of £1,000, 4 points and a discretionary disqualification.

This will not normally be charged if you have failed to provide the test initially but have proved over the limit on the station test. If you have been charged with the offence and the substantive offence it is always worth asking the prosecution if they will drop the offence of failing to co-operate with the preliminary test. If in doubt, get some initial free advice from a specialist solicitor.

There is a defence of "reasonable excuse". If you think you have a reasonable excuse you must contact a specialist solicitor because there is a great deal of case law in this area and what you may feel is a reasonable excuse is not necessarily one the law will agree with, e.g. getting bad advice from your solicitor.

It is worth taking note of the reading on a roadside breath test, because it does give an indication of the level of alcohol in your breath. This may influence whether you supply a specimen at the police station. It is advisable to supply a preliminary test for this reason and to avoid an additional charge, or any charge at all if you prove below the limit.

Since the 10th April 2015 the police do not have to request a roadside breath test and may either:

• Proceed to an evidential test if they have the appropriate device available

OR

• Proceed to arrest you if they feel they have evidence that you are under the influence of alcohol or drugs

Drugs

There is also a preliminary impairment and drug test for a person suspected of being under the influence of drugs.

Preliminary drugs test

A police officer can require a person to co-operate with a preliminary drug test, which requires a specimen of either sweat or saliva which is tested by the use of an approved device indicating the presence of a specific type of drug eg cannabis/cocaine.

Preliminary impairment test

This is known as the Romberg test and has to be administered by a trained police officer. There is a measurement of the pupils taken which, if outside the normal range of 3-6.5, is an indication that the person is affected by drugs. However, there have to be more tests satisfied.

There are:-

1. Stand still with hands by the side, tilt head back and tell the officer when you think 30 seconds has passed.

2. Walk and turn, where you are expected to walk heel to toe for 9 steps do a 180 degree turn and walk 9 steps back.

3. Stand on one leg with the other raised 6"-8" from the ground and count in terms of 1001, 1002 and then repeat the same on the other leg.

4. Finger to nose, which involves standing with arms outstretched and head tilted back and touching the tip on your nose with the tip of your finger from alternate hands.

If you fail some or all of these tests then you will be charged with the substantive offence of driving whilst unfit through drugs, assuming there is some evidence of drugs in your system. The impairment tests are likely to have become less frequent since the 5th March 2015 when the offence of driving whilst over a drugs limit comes into force. Since the 10th April 2015 the police do not have to undertake the preliminary tests if they have evidence that you are under the influence of drugs. In these circumstances they can arrest you, take you to the police station and request you to provide samples for analysis.

DRIVING/ATTEMPTING TO DRIVE WHILST UNFIT THROUGH DRINK OR DRUGS

Under S4 of the Road Traffic Act 1988 it is an offence to "drive or attempt to drive a mechanically propelled vehicle on a road or other public place whilst unfit to drive through drink or drugs". The penalty is a level 5 fine of £5,000/ unlimited for offences committed after the 12th March 2015, 6 months' imprisonment and a disqualification for at least 12 months.

APPENDIX 10 Sentencing guidelines to driving whilst unfit

If you have been disqualified for a period of 56 days or more in the preceding three years, the court must disqualify you for a period of at least two years. The court must disqualify for at least three years if you have been convicted of a drink related offence in the preceding 10 years.

"Driving"

The term driving is given its ordinary meaning but in its broadest sense. The test is that the driver is "in a substantial sense controlling the movement and direction of the car". The following circumstances have been held to be driving:-

1. Pushing and steering
2. Pushing a motorcycle whilst sat astride it
3. Engine running, driver sat in the driver's seat although not moving
4. Being towed whilst in driver's seat
5. Steering the vehicle even if not in the driver's seat

The law differs in Scotland where standing alongside a car, pushing it and leaning in to steer the car is held to be driving. The following circumstances have not been held to be driving:-

1. Engine not switched on and handbrake is released
2. Passenger awoke to find driver asleep and car moving steered it 200 yds to safety
3. During struggle in a taxi the aggressor caught the accelerator causing the taxi to drive along the road mounting the pavement.

4. Stationary at traffic lights/row of traffic.

The general test has two conditions.

1. Do you have control over the DIRECTION of the car? AND
2. Does the activity in question fall within the ordinary meaning of the word "driving"?

If you have been charged with an offence and you think that you were not driving because of the circumstances, you should always seek the advice of a specialist solicitor as there is a great deal of case law on the subject and as you can see from the examples mentioned above, it is not always obvious.

"Attempt"

Attempting to drive is a question of degree. The test is how far you have gone without actually driving the vehicle. The legal test is that you must have done "more than what is merely preparatory". Examples are:-

1. Sitting in the driver's seat and turning the engine on
2. Pushing a motorcycle to the junction from a private highway to a public road
3. In the driver's seat trying to put the keys into the ignition
4. Trying to start a vehicle when it has broken down and cannot be started

Whether you are attempting to drive is a question of degree. Even if you fall within one of the examples above, there may be evidence which can establish that you were not going to drive and therefore were not attempting to drive. You must remember that even if for some mechanical reason the car will not start, you could still be held to be attempting to drive if that was your intention. In reality it is unusual to be prosecuted for attempting to drive because it can be difficult to prove. If you are in a car attempting to drive you will almost certainly be found guilty of being "in charge" of a vehicle so the police favour the latter charge to the former. The prosecution will prove the offence of being unfit through drugs by the impairment test and a full analysis of your blood for drugs. It is unusual to see the offence charged for unfit through drink offences, because the police will usually go through the excess alcohol procedure, and the penalties for failing to provide are equally high so the police prefer S5 offences when dealing with alcohol offences. I suspect the same will happen with the new drug charge which came on the 5th March 2015. If you do give a blood sample, remember to retain yours and seek specialist advice immediately. If in doubt, do not admit to driving in any way. Just go through the procedure and leave any arguments for another day after seeking advice.

IN CHARGE WHILST UNFIT THROUGH DRINK OR DRUGS.

It is an offence to be "in charge" of a vehicle whilst unfit through drink or drugs. The preliminary tests are the same as the substantive charge of driving/attempting to drive. The penalty is a Level 4 fine of £2,500, 3 months' imprisonment, 10 points or a discretionary disqualification.

APPENDIX 11 Sentencing guidelines to Being In Charge Whilst Unfit.

The key issue is when you would be held to be in charge. You will be held to be in charge if:-

1.   You are the owner of the vehicle and the vehicle has been recently driven.
2.   You have taken control of the vehicle voluntarily.
The relevant factors to consider are:-
1.   Where were you in the vehicle?
2.   How far were you from the vehicle?
3.   What were you doing at the relevant time?
4.   Were you in possession of the ignition key?
5.   Did you have the intention to take or assert control over the vehicle, driving or otherwise?

For example, a man left asleep in the passenger seat of the car outside his brother's house by his wife was held not to be in charge after appeal. It will be a defence to show that you had no intention to drive whilst unfit or, in the case of an S5 offence, whilst over the limit. This will need to be established on a balance of probabilities, which is basically more likely than not. However, to show that you would have been fit to drive or not over the limit you will have to have some "compelling evidence" or expert scientific evidence which, by calculation, shows that you would be under the limit or no longer affected by drugs or alcohol. Sleeping it off with the intention of driving in the early morning will not usually be sufficient, because you would not be certain that you were not still over the limit or affected by drugs, as it would all depend on the speed at which your body has been able to eliminate the alcohol or drug. It is worthy of note that drugs take much longer to eliminate from your system than alcohol. Any damage or mechanical defect to your vehicle will be ignored much in the same way as attempt, because the court will apply the "but for intervention" rule.

In other words, but for the vehicle having broken down, you would have driven.

DRIVING WITH EXCESS ALCOHOL

This is a very serious offence, which carries up to 6 months' imprisonment and/or a fine of £5,000/unlimited for offences committed after the 12th March 2015 as well as an obligatory disqualification of 12 months; three years if you have been convicted of a previous drink driving offence within the last 10 years. Two years' disqualification if you have two previous disqualifications of more than 56 days in the previous three years.

APPENDIX 12 Sentencing guidelines for Driving with Excess Alcohol

You will be charged if your readings are above:-

Breath 35mg in 100ml
Blood 80mg in 100ml
Urine 107mg in 100ml

You will normally be required to provide a specimen of breath. The procedure cannot be delayed to seek the advice of a solicitor. You will only be required to supply specimens of blood or urine if you have medical reasons for not supplying a breath specimen or a machine is not available for you to supply a breath specimen. You should raise any medical issues at the time of being asked to provide a specimen. This also applies if you have a phobia of needles and are asked to supply a specimen of blood. Note this has to be a genuine phobia and not a dislike of needles. If you have piercings and tattoos, establishing a phobia will be much more difficult and you could be charged with failing to provide a specimen. It is the decision of the police officer whether you supply a specimen of blood or urine. There is a presumption that the proportion of alcohol at the time of the offence is not less than the certificate of analysis, but not if you prove you consumed alcohol after you had stopped driving AND that if you had not done so, the proportion of alcohol would not have exceeded the prescribed limit. It is commonly known as the "hip flask" defence. This is difficult to prove because an expert report has two sections: what is the level of alcohol prior to driving based on your submissions as to what you drank before driving, AND does the quantity of alcohol you drank after plus what you drank before equate to the level of alcohol recorded.

If you are not telling the truth about what you have drunk before and after driving, unless you are able to do the calculations, it is likely the levels will not match and this makes it very difficult to prove that what you are saying about what you drank is true. Sometimes it can be slightly out and that is more arguable because after all none us particularly keep a record of what we have drunk. If you have evidence of post drive drinking retain it i.e. a bottle. The police will normally ask you to mark the quantity you drank on the bottle. It is possible to defend the charge if, for example, you can establish that you were not driving, or it was not a public place/road. It may also be possible to show that the reading/analysis is unreliable as often procedures are not followed or equipment is faulty.

Special Reasons

If you accept that you are guilty of driving with excess alcohol you may be able to avoid a disqualification by arguing that special reasons apply in your case.

Examples of special reasons are:-

• Laced drinks
• Short distance driven
• Emergency/necessity

This is an area of law riddled with case law as to what amounts to a special reason, and it is always preferable to seek the advice of a road traffic specialist such as Auriga Advocates who provide free initial advice. (See Chapter 16)

IN CHARGE WITH EXCESS ALCOHOL

The same principles apply for being "in charge" as previously discussed in the "in charge whilst unfit" charges. The sentence, if convicted of being in charge of a vehicle with excess alcohol, is up to 3 months' imprisonment, £2,500 fine, a discretionary disqualification and if not imposed, 10 penalty points.

APPENDIX 13 Sentencing guidelines for In charge with Excess Alcohol

DRIVING WITH EXCESS DRUGS

On the 2nd March 2015, a new law came into effect which introduced offences for drug driving. The current drug driving legislation requires the presence of drugs and evidence of impairment, which is often difficult for the police to prove. The new law will work on the same principles as the drink driving offences with specified levels and excess will result in prosecution. The offence will carry a mandatory disqualification and a maximum of 6 months' imprisonment or a level 5 fine of £5,000/unlimited for offences committed after the 12th March 2015. Being in charge with excess drugs will result in a fine of £2,500 and/ or 3 months and 10 points/discretionary disqualification.

The police will use a drug screening device (DSD) to establish the presence of drugs. These can test up to 6 drugs in a single test of a person's saliva. These is only one DSD approved so far, and it is only approved for cannabis presence.

The DSDs are not 100% accurate and therefore cannot be used as evidence in a court case. They can give false readings both positive and negative, and are affected by eating and drinking prior to the test, which is why manufacturers of the DSD recommend that there should be a 10 minute delay after eating or drinking.

The Crime and Courts Act 2013 created a new limits-based offence of drug-driving by inserting a new section 5A in the Road Traffic Act 1988. Under the Act, a driver can be convicted if "the proportion of the drug in" his or her "blood or urine exceeds the specified limit for that drug".

The drug limits are as follows:-

Illicit drugs
- Benzoylecgonine, 50 µg/L
- Cocaine, 10 µg/L
- Delta–9–Tetrahydrocannabinol (Cannabis and Cannabinol), 2 µg/L
- Ketamine, 20 µg/L
- Lysergic Acid Diethylamide (LSD), 1 µg/L
- Methylamphetamine – 10 µg/L
- Methylenedioxymethaphetamine (MDMA – Ecstasy), 10 µg/L

- 6-Monoacetylmorphine (6-MAM – Heroin and Morphine), 5 µg/L

Generally Prescription Drugs
- Clonazepam, 50 µg/L
- Diazepam, 550 µg/L
- Flunitrazepam, 300 µg/L
- Lorazepam, 100 µg/L
- Methadone, 500 µg/L
- Morphine, 80 µg/L
- Oxazepam, 300 µg/L
- Temazepam, 1000 µg/L

There are still a number of concerns about whether the limits accurately reflect the different speeds at which the drug breaks down in the blood, but the assurances have been provided that the limits include these variations.

Some prescribed drugs could give positive results for illicit drugs, e.g. dexamphetamine which is used to treat ADHD sufferers, or Sativex which is used to treat MS sufferers. Both drugs could give positive results for amphetamine or cannabis. However a defence has been introduced under S5 A(3) which states that if a drug is prescribed for medical or dental reasons and taken in accordance with any directions by the doctor, dentist or consultant and also the manufacturer's instructions. The drugs must also be being used legally i.e. not prescribed to another person.

Until more devices are approved which can measure accurately the levels, the police will still be required to do the impairment test which is currently mandatory for driving whilst unfit through drugs.

There are similar offences of "being in charge" and failing to supply specimens which carry similar penalties.

FAILING TO PROVIDE A SPECIMEN

If you refuse to provide a specimen of any type at the police station, you will be charged with the offence of failing to provide a specimen for analysis. This will also be charged if you have apparently tried, but failed, to provide the specimen without a reasonable excuse. What amounts to a reasonable excuse in law will not be obvious to you, as there is case law defining what amounts to a reasonable excuse. Trying your best and failing will not amount to a reasonable excuse.

The penalties vary in relation to this offence depend on whether you were driving/attempting to drive or were "in charge". For an offence committed whilst driving/ attempting to drive, the penalty is a level 5 fine which is unlimited for offences committed after the 12th March 2015 and/or 6 months' imprisonment, as well as a mandatory disqualification for a minimum of 12 months.

For an offence committed whilst "in charge" the penalty is a level 4 fine of £2,500 and/or 3 months, a discretionary disqualification or 10 points.

WHAT DO I DO IF I AM CHARGED WITH A DRINK/DRUG RELATED OFFENCE?

Drink driving offences are very difficult to deal with without representation due to the complexity of the issues, which are often very technical as well. Even if you are intending to plead guilty, you would best advised to seek both advice and representation from a specialist solicitor. Most specialist solicitors will give you some initial advice free over the telephone.

If you attend court you will get the opportunity to get some free advice and representation from the duty solicitor.

There are a number of difficulties with this:-

- Duty solicitor will have a number of cases to deal with
- Less time is spent on your case
- Little preparation as a result
- Duty solicitor cannot represent you for trial; you would have to apply for legal aid (which is unlikely to be granted if you are above a basic income)
- You may instruct another solicitor so you would lose any consistency in representation.
- The duty solicitor may offer to represent you privately, but it is unlikely that you would get the same solicitor to represent you in court
- Duty solicitor is not an expert in road traffic.

It is for these reasons that you will always get better and more effective representation from a specialist solicitor such as Auriga Advocates where you will receive the time, attention and expertise that your case deserves.

Chapter Twelve
Driving Whilst
Disqualified

There are three types of disqualification which can be ordered by the court.

- Mandatory for the offence
- Discretionary for the offence
- Mandatory under the totting up procedure

If an offence carries a disqualification or you are facing a totting disqualification, you may consider trying to avoid the imposition of the disqualification or points by pleading Special Reasons or Exceptional Hardship (see Chapter 16). Once imposed, it is a court order and any breach is dealt with harshly by the court.

S103 Road Traffic Act 1988 makes it an offence, whilst disqualified, to:

- Hold or obtain a driving licence
- Drive a motor vehicle on a road

The penalty is a level 5 fine of £5,000 or unlimited fine for offences committed after the 12th March 2015/6 months' imprisonment and a discretionary disqualification or an endorsement on your driving record of 6 points.

APPENDIX 14 Sentencing guidelines for disqualified driving.

The prosecution must prove that:
a) you were driving
AND
b) you were disqualified.

Proving that you were driving can be difficult. The definition for driving is the same as outlined in Chapter 11. If the police have stopped you in the vehicle it can be easily proved.However, if they have merely seen you in the vehicle and arrested you later or when they get to the vehicle after you have left it, you may be able to challenge the identification of the driver. If the police know you well, it will be a case of recognition as opposed to identification. If identification is challenged, they must hold an identification parade but often do not, which can lead to legal challenges and submissions which only qualified expert solicitors should do, as it would extremely difficult for a non-lawyer to do well.

The second point to prove is that you were disqualified. This is easier as they can produce certificates of the disqualification (known as memorandum of conviction), a confession by you or from the evidence of a person present at the court where you were convicted i.e. a legal advisor. Sometimes you can challenge the conviction in which case the prosecution would have to prove that the person disqualified was you, and this can be achieved by fingerprint evidence. I have had cases where it appears that there ought to be a re-test after the period of disqualification and the person driving would, therefore, be disqualified until such time as they have taken the re-test. I have requested the court extract, which is the court's record of the hearing when that person was convicted, and although they should have ordered the re-test, they had not; therefore that person was not guilty of driving whilst disqualified, because his disqualification finished after the disqualification period and not after a re-test.

If you do not accept that you were disqualified you should seek the advice and representation of a specialist solicitor.

A DISQUALIFICATION UNTIL RE-TEST/ EXTENDED RE-TEST

Under S36 of the Road Traffic Offenders Act 1988, the court can order a disqualification until such time as a further driving test is undertaken (re-test); for some offences, they can impose an extended re-test. If you are disqualified with a re-test you will remain disqualified from driving until that test it taken. You can drive after the disqualification period, but that will be as a provisional driver and as such you can only apply for your provisional licence before you start any driving. When you do drive, you must comply with all the provisional driver provisions outlined in chapter 4; failure to do so will mean that you are driving whilst disqualified. You should also ensure that you are in possession of your provisional licence.

DISQUALIFICATION UNDER THE "TOTTING UP" PROCEDURE

Once you have acquired 12 points or more, you will be disqualified initially for a period of 6 months and this period will increase if you "tot" again, i.e. 12 months for a second disqualification under the "totting up" procedure. These disqualifications have the effect of "wiping the slate clean" as they remove all previous points, provided the disqualification is for longer than 56 days. This is not the case with a period of disqualification imposed for the offence.

You count the endorsements from the date of the earliest offence to the date of the offences; within a three year period, if that adds to 12 or more points, you will be liable to be disqualified. It is a complicated calculation when you have a disqualification on your driving record. Here are a few examples to assist:-

Example 1.

Offence	Date of Offence	Sentence
Dangerous Condition	1.1.12	3 points
Tyre	1.9.13	3 points
Careless Driving	1.7.14	5 points
No Insurance	1.12.14	

The offender has 3 offences in the previous three years and has totalled 11 points. The offence of speeding carries 3-6 points so even if 3 points were imposed, the offender would be eligible for a "totting" disqualification.

Example 2.

Offence	Date of Offence	Sentence	Date of Conviction
Speeding	1.1.12	3 points	2.4.12
Failure to Stop	1.7.12	5 points	5.9.12
No Insur-ance	1.9.13	Disqualified 6 mths TT99	2.11.13
Careless driving	1.12.14		

The offender would have 8 points on his licence, and ordinarily he would be eligible to be disqualified for careless driving if ordered 4 points or more; however, TT99 shows that the disqualification on the 2.11.2013 has removed the previous points, so if the court awarded 4 points he would only have 4 points on his licence, and disqualification under totting would not be considered. Disqualification for the offence itself may be (unlikely if they are only awarding 4 points which would suggest lower level of due care).

Example 3.

Offence	Date of Offence	Sentence	Date of Conviction
Speeding	1.1.11	3 points	4.3.12
Careless Driving	1.7.12	Disqualification 3 mths for offence	13.9.13
Speeding	31.3.14	6 points	26.6.14
Tyre	1.12.14		

A tyre offence carries 3 points. The previous disqualification was for the offence andtherefore does not wipe the slate clean, so the points prior to the disqualification are still on the record; so he is "totting", and would be eligible for a disqualification.

Example 4.

Offence	Date of Offence	Sentence	Date of Conviction
Defective Light	1.1.11	3 points	1.9.11
Tyre	1.4.11	3 points	1.12.11
No Insurance	30.3.13	6 points	(1.12.14)
Speeding	2.2.13	3 points	3.10.13

In this example the court has to sentence the offender for the no insurance after the expiry of 3 years, but the court has to consider the offences as of the date of offence so the no insurance would fall within the three year period from date of offence to date of offence – so would be eligible for disqualification.

The court must impose the minimum period unless "having regard to all the circumstances there are no grounds for mitigating the normal consequences of a conviction". The court will not take into account any of the following grounds:

- any grounds alleged to make the offence less serious
- hardship other than exceptional hardship; and

• any circumstances taken into account by a court when the offender escaped disqualification or was disqualified for less than the minimum period on a previous occasion within the three years preceding the current conviction, when he was liable to be disqualified under the totting up procedure.

The argument which can be considered is "exceptional hardship", although the court can take into account any other mitigating circumstances which do not fall into the exceptions above. (For further details on pleading "exceptional hardship" see Chapter 16)

REDUCTION OF A DRINK DRIVING DISQUALIFICATION

If you have been convicted of a drink driving related offence and disqualified for 12 months or more you may be offered a Drink Drivers' Rehabilitation Course which will reduce your disqualification period by 25 %. The courses are designed to address attitudes to drink driving and therefore reduce the risk of further drink driving. Evidence shows that those who have attended the course are 3 times less likely to re-offend than those who do not.

If offered the course at court you will be asked which course provider you wish to do the course with. You will have been given details of the providers and their prices prior to the hearing. The cost varies from area to area but a rough guide would be between £150-£250.

The court will give you details as to when you need to complete the course by and the level of reduction. The longer your disqualification, the greater the reduction, so if you are disqualified for 24 months, your disqualification could be reduced by 6 months.

Once completed, you will receive a certificate which will need to be sent to the DVLA and the record for the period of disqualification will be amended. Once this period has elapsed you can apply for your driving licence. You should not drive until in receipt of your licence. If the course provider refuses to give you a certificate, he must give you a written notice of his decision within 14 days of the end of the course. You can then apply to the supervising court for a declaration that the organiser's decision was contrary to the requirements of the statute. I would get a solicitor to do this for you, most will for a small fee.

The course will not be offered a second time within a three year period of you completing a previous course. It will not be offered to a driver in their probationary period.

REMOVAL OF A DISQUALIFICATION

The court has the power to remove a disqualification on the following grounds:

1. If the disqualification is less than four years, and two years from the date it was imposed have expired.
2. If the disqualification is less than 10 years, but more than four years if half of the period has expired.
3. In any other cases i.e. 10 years or more then five years must have expired.

If the disqualification is less than two years you cannot apply and therefore your only option would be to appeal against sentence (see Chapter 16). You can apply if you have a mandatory three year disqualification after a second offence.

However, it is not always easy to get a disqualification removed early. If you fall within the criteria above, you can apply in writing to both the court and the Chief Officer of Police for your local area (you can usually find these details easily from their websites).

The application should include the following details:-

• Details about the offence, date of offence
• Date and period of disqualification (be careful to check if an interim disqualification was imposed because this will pre-date the sentencing date)
• Reasons why the court should remove the disqualification

The court may remove a disqualification if it feels it is appropriate to do so after having given proper regards to the following:

Applicant's character	Providing a character reference would assist your case or getting them to give evidence in court. Providing evidence of what you have done since which reflects a good positive law abiding attitude
Conduct since the conviction	This means that you should not have any convictions of any kind since the disqualification. If you do, you should be able to offer an explanation as to why it can be ignored.

	Generally this will only work for minor offences and not more serious offences. Any work or activities which demonstrate good behaviour i.e. volunteering, employment or work experience
Nature of the Offence	The more serious the offence, the less likely the court are to remove the disqualification and the stronger the two former grounds will need to be to try and persuade them
Any other circumstances	This could be anything such as the reasons you need to be able to drive e.g. to secure employment/ assist a disabled dependant.

Lord Widgery provided guidance for the magistrates' court where an offender applied for removal of a mandatory disqualification, such a three year disqualification due to a second drink driving offence within 10 years.

"… May if they think fit… regard a mandatory disqualification as one which they are somewhat less ready to remove than a discretionary one."

The upshot of this is that the Magistrates do not often remove such a disqualification without exceptionally strong grounds.

You cannot apply just because it is a special birthday ie 50 years.

Although this is something that you could undertake yourself, I would advise that you at least secure some advice from a specialist solicitor such as Auriga Advocates who will give the initial advice free. Due to the reluctance to remove disqualifications, you must be confident that you can write a good case and acquire your supporting evidence; if not, to have any chance of success you should instruct a solicitor. Most specialist solicitors offer a fixed fee rate for this type of work in the region of £250-350 for a written representation and £500 for court representation.

Chapter Thirteen
Parking

Parking issues are frequently in the news due to the extortionate rates that some private parking enforcement companies charge. You must distinguish between a public authority enforcing a parking regulation, which amounts to an offence, and a private body who is merely enforcing a civil contract.

WHEEL CLAMPS

Since 1st October 2012 under the Protection of Freedoms Act 2012 S54, if a person without lawful authority immobilises a motor vehicle on private land by the attachment of an immobilising device (clamp) to all or part of it, or moves or restricts the movement of any such vehicle by any means, commits an offence. The penalty is a fine at level 5: £5,000.

Persons with lawful authority are local authorities, the DVLA and the police. When someone with lawful authority does clamp a vehicle your vehicle the "clamper" must provide you with a receipt detailing:-

- place
- name and signature of clamper
- licence number
- date

The person clamping must be displaying their licence. You must not damage any clamp which is lawfully placed. There must be warning signs in place. Only a reasonable fee can be charged and must provide immediate release. There should be no delay on release after payment is made. There should be a clear way to communicate to get released.

Since the clamping on private land has been illegal there should be fewer issues, and if you are clamped on private land you should call the police because it is an offence. Do not get into arguments with the clampers, who may become very threatening, and if so you should call the police immediately.

TOWING YOUR VEHICLE

The police and traffic wardens have the power to remove a vehicle. They have to provide 24 hours' notice and you can claim it within 7 days. This includes when a vehicle:-

- has broken down
- is causing an obstruction
- is causing a danger
- is a potential danger

It is an offence to try to interfere with the removal of your vehicle as it will be the "wilful obstruction of a traffic officer".

The police or local authority can retain the vehicle until there has been a payment of a removal fee, which is on a sliding scale depending on the size and condition of the vehicle, e.g. less than 3.5 tonnes and undamaged is £150, going up to £6,000 for much larger vehicles, damaged vehicles, loaded vehicles. There will also be a storage charge of £10-35 per day, depending again on the size and condition of the vehicle. The fees can only be paid by the vehicle owner.

PARKING TICKETS

There is a distinction between private companies and public bodies.

Public Bodies

Public bodies such as the local authority or the police can enforce parking tickets. If the council are part of the DPE (decriminalised parking enforcement) they will have an appeals service independent from the court, if not they will be enforced via the county court.

If you are issued with a parking ticket you should check that all the details are present to the vehicle, time, date and place of parking as well as details as to who to contact and the person issuing the parking ticket (PCN).

There are several grounds upon which you can challenge a parking ticket:

- Information on the ticket is wrong
- Did not own the vehicle (posted PCN)
- Loading/unloading
- Exceptional circumstances
- Compelling reasons

You should put your challenge in writing with clear, concise and structured arguments. The layout should be as follows:-

Reference : Ticket number – time, date and place of issue

Paragraph 1. Outline the circumstance in which you were parked. (i.e. how you got there, why you were parked)

Paragraph 2. Identify the circumstances of your defence i.e. loading/unloading with reference to any photographic/ other evidence you have in support.

Paragraph 3. Conclude – summarising your defence and asking them to withdraw the parking ticket.

Retain a copy of your letter and also any evidence in support. You could get a solicitor to write a letter for you, but in light of the low fines imposed for parking it would not be very cost effective. You could, of course, call a specialist for initial free advice to get an idea of what you should put in a letter.

If your challenge is not accepted you can appeal; if you do so within the 14 day discounted period, you will still have the opportunity to accept the discounted fine if your challenge fails. You actually have up to 28 days to challenge the ticket, but if you do it after the 14 days you lose your discounted entitlement.

If you are parked somewhere that you know could cause problems i.e. permit zones, if loading or unloading take photographs before and after and put a notice in your vehicle stating that you are loading/unloading. Take a photograph of the sign in situ. If you have any delivery notes etc keep those to attach to your challenge. You should get as much evidence that supports your argument as possible. This could be documents, statements, photographs of signage and many others. If you seek initial advice from a solicitor they will be able to advise free of charge as to what evidence would be good support.

Private Parking

Private parking could be at a supermarket, shopping centre or hospital. Usually it will be very clear from the signage that the car park is not ran by the local authority. In these cases there is no offence of parking, as the matter is civil only. The use of the word penalty in both signage and tickets is misleading.

Parking in these circumstances comes under contract law. In a contract there must be the following to have an enforceable contract:-

1. Offer
2. Acceptance
3. Clear terms and conditions.

The terms and conditions should be clear upon entry to the car park as it is arguable that by entering the car park, once parked, you have accepted the offer to park there. Any terms and conditions in a position after you have entered would more than likely be deemed unenforceable because you had already concluded the contract.

If the car park has no notices at all, any attempt to enforce penalties will be invalid and unenforceable.

However, many car parks are ran by very well organised companies who have numerous signs in place so it could be difficult to say you had not seen them. But the terms and conditions themselves have to be fair to be enforceable. Penalty clauses have to be reasonable and be only calculated to cover actual loss. It could be arguable that most car park penalties therefore will always be unreasonable, because potentially the loss incurred will depend entirely on the circumstances, i.e. how busy the car park was, how long the period of parking beyond the time limit etc.

If the terms and conditions are misleading they will be unenforceable and invalid. The so called fixed penalty notice that these companies send out or attach to your car are really a claim for compensation due to a breach of contract and are not a fine, as they are designed to make you believe so that you will pay without question.

The real question is: do you have to pay it? If all the terms and conditions are clear and you knew them before parking, then potentially yes. But you must consider what the loss is to the landowner and whether the compensation they are asking for covers that loss. It should not cover more. In contract law, an injured party should do all in their power to mitigate their loss. So if there are a lot of parking spaces available, they will not have suffered any loss at all because any other vehicle coming onto the car park could park. The only time they would suffer loss is if you had prevented another vehicle from parking and paying the fee.

In calculating whether the fee requested is reasonable, you should consider the parking charge, e.g. £1.00 per hour, and then multiply that by the time that you parked when not covered by your payment. Some car parks are free for a specific period of time but then impose fees for overstaying; the question you need to ask in such cases is: has there been any loss at all?

Defences to raise with the parking company:-

- I did not break the rules
- There were no signs/signs were misleading (take photographs)
- Signs were located after the contract was concluded
- Fees requested are unreasonable as they do not appear to reflect the actual loss (take photographs of the car park to show spaces available, clock to show times involved)
- The time over limit was so short as to be "de minimis" and cannot be held to be a breach.
- I was not the person who parked the car – note that you do not have to disclose who was parking to a private company.
- I had a good reason to park as I did e.g. appointment overran at the hospital.

You should structure the letter much the same as the letter to a council when challenging a parking notice. Always include the evidence such as photographs. Always ask them to produce evidence of how long you had paid for, if time is the issue, and ask them for evidence of the actual loss incurred to prove that the fees they are asking for are "reasonable".

You will usually get a further letter with threats to increase the penalty. Some companies are members of parking associations such as the British Parking Association or the Independent Parking Committee. An appeal can go to them but has no validity at all because they cannot enforce the contract. I have had experience of parking companies providing inaccurate evidence, such as stating that the time paid for was less than actually was paid for, to show that the time was overspent by an hour rather than few minutes. You should request all the evidence as soon as you get the ticket so that you can counter these sort of actions at this appeal stage. More often than not, the companies are supported.

However, keep going as the company cannot enforce the fees without taking you to the county court. It is expensive to do this and most are reluctant as a result. If they do go to court then, if you have followed the advice above, you should already have your defence case to present. It will be dealt with at a small claims court which is less formal and geared for people who are unrepresented. Note that if you lose, it is likely that you will face court and legal costs of the parking company, but if you have followed this advice to the letter you should have a strong case.

However, a word of caution: there is an appeal case awaiting the decision called Beavis which was heard at the appeal court on the 24th February 2015. Their decision was announced on the 23rd April 2015 and Mr Beavis's appeal was dismissed. This means that at the moment, penalties in the sum of £85 are "not extravagant or unconscionable" and the charge was "neither improper in its purpose nor manifestly excessive in amount". At present, if your only argument is that the charge is excessive and unreasonable, I would suggest that it is likely you will lose the argument in light of the court of appeal decision in Beavis.

So you are well advised to keep an eye on this case and read the judgement when it is published. The decision will assist you in reaching a decision as to whether to accept or defend a penalty. This does take some nerve to keep going and not break under the pressure and threats of these companies, which is exactly what they rely on.

There are a number of other offences related to parking which you should be aware of.

PARKING AT NIGHT

It is an offence to allow a motor vehicle to stand on any road between sunset and sunrise otherwise than with its left or nearside as close as it may be to the edge of the carriageway.

Except:

• With the permission of a police officer in uniform
• Fire and rescue, police, defence, ambulances in such circumstances where it would hinder the use of the vehicle, or likely to hinder the use of the vehicle for which it is being used on that occasion.
• Vehicles on building work, repair work/road work, removing traffic obstructions, but only if compliance of the regulations would hinder or be likely to hinder the use of the vehicle.
• One-way streets, and
• Car parks, taxi stands and bus stops if to follow the regulations would cause problems for the vehicle.

PARKING ON GRASS VERGES

It is an offence for heavy commercial vehicles to park on verges, footpaths or central reservations. A heavy commercial vehicle is one exceeding 7.5 tonnes operating weight. The wheels must be touching the road surface to be in breach of this regulation.

It is a defence if:-

• Loading/unloading on footway or verge and it could only be satisfactorily performed by being parked in such a way.
• Parked with the permission of the police, lifesaving, firefighting or other emergency.

LEAVING A VEHICLE IN A DANGEROUS POSITION

It is an offence if you are in charge of a vehicle to cause or permit the vehicle, or trailer drawn by it, to remain at rest on road in such a position or in such condition involve a danger of injury to other persons using the road.

The penalty is a level 3 fine of £1,000, discretionary disqualification or 3 points.

There has to be a danger or injury and that danger can arise either whilst it is stationary or when the vehicle is moved. Examples are: parking on a bend, humpbacked bridge.

The danger must be to other road users and not to occupants of a building, so blocking an exit from a fire station would not be an offence under this regulation, but of course could be an offence of obstruction.

OBSTRUCTING THE HIGHWAY OR ROAD

There are three ways in which you can obstruct a highway:-

• Cause/permit a vehicle to cause unnecessary obstruction: Reg 103 Road Vehicle (Construction and Use) Regulations 1986
• Wilfully cause an obstruction on a public footpath or thoroughfare to the annoyance or danger of residents: S28 Town and Police Clauses Act 1847
• Wilfully obstruct free passage along the highway: S137 Highways Act 1980

There are a number of factors which have to be considered to establish whether or not there is an obstruction:-

• length of time vehicle is parked

- the location of the vehicle
- the purpose for which it is parked
- whether there is actual or potential obstruction

Actual case examples where there has been held to be an obstruction are:-
- Doing a U-turn in a busy street holding traffic up for 50 seconds
- Parking next to a bus stop for 5 minutes and refusing to move
- Parking close to another vehicle and refusing to move to allow another vehicle to move
- Parking a hot dog van on a busy road to sell hot dogs.

"WILFUL AND UNNECESSARY"

This requirement in the offence means that in some way the obstruction must be deliberate, so if your vehicle has broken down it would not be deliberate; but if you left it without making arrangements to get it moved as soon as possible, then it would be considered to be deliberate.

ABANDONING A VEHICLE/UNAUTHORISED DUMPING

Under S2(1) of the Refuse (amenity) Act 1978 it is an offence if without lawful authority to abandon on land in open air/any other land forming part of the highway a motor vehicle or anything which formed part of a motor vehicle and was removed from it in the course of dismantling the vehicle on the land commits an offence. Otherwise known as "fly tipping".

The local authority has the power to remove any vehicle which appears abandoned. The term abandoned is given its ordinary meaning "give up, desert, leave permanently". The local authority are entitled to recover the costs of removal in addition to any penalty imposed for the offence. The offence carries a level 4 fine £2,500/3 months' imprisonment.

Appendix 15 Schedule of parking offence and penalties

Chapter Fourteen
Pedestrian Crossing

There are several types of crossing:

• Zebra
• Pelican/puffin
• Toucan – for cyclists as well as pedestrians
• Pegasus – horses

All have "controlled areas" and "crossing limits". The distinction is important as there are specific offences in relation to each.

A controlled area is the whole of the crossing from beginning to the end of the zigzag markings.

A crossing limit is the area within the inner most line of studs or the white stripe on the edge of the crossing if there are no studs (zebra) and the in case of other types of crossing within the stud marks.

It is an offence to stop within the "crossing limits" unless prevented from proceeding in circumstances beyond your control or to prevent injury to a person. The penalty is a level 3 fine £1,000, a discretionary disqualification or 3 points.

Exemptions are fire and rescue, ambulance, building works, road works and emergencies. Running out of petrol will not be a defence as it is something within your control, however breaking down due to an unknown defect may be.

It is also an offence for a pedestrian to remain on the carriageway within the crossing limits for longer than is reasonably necessary. The penalty is a level 3 fine £1,000.

It is an offence to stop your vehicle wholly or in part in the controlled area except:-

- When giving precedence to a pedestrian
- Unable to avoid due to circumstances beyond your control
- Police, fire, ambulance
- As long as is necessary for vehicle is required to stop for building work, removing obstruction, road works or maintenance of utilities.
- PSV on local service picking up or alighting passengers
- Turning left or right

It is an offence to overtake another vehicle within the controlled area or to fail to comply with the light system at a crossing. The penalty is a level 3 fine £1,000, discretionary disqualification or 3 points. (Band A Fine).

Precedence is given to a pedestrian who has entered the crossing limits so a vehicle must stop. Failure to do so is an offence. The same applies to pelican crossings when the lights are flashing amber, so if a pedestrian has stepped onto the crossing limits you must allow them to cross.

A crossing must conform with the regulations before any offence can be committed. However if there is a non-compliance of these regulations, as long as the general appearance of the crossing and its controls are operating, then it will not amount to a material breach and the crossing will be legal for the purposes of offences in relation to it. These can be found in the Zebra Pelican and Puffin

Pedestrian Crossings Regulation and General Directions 1997 9 (as amended).

SCHOOL CROSSINGS

A driver must stop when the stop sign is shown by the traffic patrol "lollipop man" and in a manner which does not impede the person crossing, and remain stationary for so long as the sign is exhibited. The traffic patrol officer must be in uniform. The penalty is a level 3 fine £1,000, a discretionary disqualification or a 3 points.

Chapter Fifteen
Miscellaneous Offences

This chapter covers numerous other offences which you should be aware of. Any reference to a regulation will be referring to the Road Vehicle (Construction and Use) Regulations 1986 unless otherwise specified.

DRIVING ON FOOTWAY/COMMON LAND/ PRIVATE ROAD

Under the S72 of the Highways Act 1835 it is an offence to wilfully ride or drive on a footway; this also includes horses, asses, mules, swine, a carriage, truck or sledge. The penalty is a level 2 fine of £500.

S34 of the Road Traffic Act 1988 prohibits the driving a mechanically propelled vehicle on footpaths, bridle ways, restricted byways, common land, moorland, or other land not forming part of the road, except for emergencies or parking within 15 yards of a road in order to park.

The onus is on the driver to prove the exception. (see Appendix 15)

VEHICLES USED IN MANNER CAUSING ALARM, DISTRESS OR ANNOYANCE

Where a constable in uniform has reasonable grounds for believing that a motor vehicle is being used on any occasion in a manner which:-

• contravenes section 3 or 34 of the Road Traffic Act 1988 (c. 52) (careless and inconsiderate driving and prohibition of off-road driving), and

• is causing, or is likely to cause, alarm, distress or annoyance to members of the public

The constable has the following powers:-

• power, if the motor vehicle is moving, to order the person driving it to stop the vehicle;

• power to seize and remove the motor vehicle;

• power, for the purposes of exercising a power falling within paragraph (a) or (b), to enter any premises on which he has reasonable grounds for believing the motor vehicle to be;

• power to use reasonable force, if necessary, in the exercise of any power

An officer cannot seize a motor vehicle unless he has warned the person committing the offence and the person has continued that use or repeated it. He does not have to give the warning if it is impracticable for him to do so, or if he has already given a warning to that person or another regarding the use of that vehicle or another, or if he believes a warning has previously been given by another officer, or if he has reasonable grounds for believing that the person whose use of that motor vehicle on that occasion would justify the seizure is a person to whom a warning under that subsection has been given on a previous occasion in the previous twelve months.

The penalty of failing to comply with an order is a level 3 fine of £1,000.

QUITTING A VEHICLE

It is an offence to leave or cause or permit a motor vehicle to be left on a road unattended by a person licensed to drive it, unless the engine has stopped and the brake is set or it is a fire engine at work or a gas driven vehicle or is being used for police or ambulance services.

You will be classed to have left a vehicle unattended if you are asleep in it with the engine running and the brake off.

You will still be guilty of the offence if the vehicle was left on private land but rolls onto a road. It is a defence to show that there has been an intervention by a 3rd party.

It is also an offence to leave a vehicle with the engine running so far as reasonably necessary for the prevention of noise except for examination of the vehicle, working for other purposes and gas propelled vehicles.

NEGLIGENT OPENING OF CAR DOORS

It is an offence to open a car door so as to injure or endanger any person. The penalty is a level 3 fine of £1,000.

MUD DEPOSITING AND OTHER MATTERS ON A HIGHWAY

It is an offence to deposit anything whatsoever on a highway without lawful authority, whereby use of the highway has caused injury or a person would be endangered. The prosecution must prove that injury was caused or there is a danger of injury. The penalty is a level 3 fine £1,000.

It is also an offence to allow dirt, lime, or other offensive matter or thing to run or flow on to a highway from an adjoining premises without lawful authority. The penalty is a level 1 fine of £200.

Lighting a fire on or over a carriageway or discharging a firearm or firework within 50 ft of the centre of a carriageway and consequently injuring, interrupting or endangering a user of the highway is an offence which carries a level 3 fine of £1,000.

PLAYING FOOTBALL IN THE HIGHWAY

Playing football or any other games on a highway to the annoyance of a user of the highway is an offence which carries a level 2 fine of £500.

SKIPS ON A ROAD

Before a skip can be deposited on a road, the permission of the local authority must be obtained and the skip owner must comply with the conditions such as being lit at night, display clearly the name address and telephone number of the skip owner on the side. The skip must be removed as soon as practicable after it is full. Failure to do so is an offence which carries a level 3 fine of £1,000.

It is a defence if you can show that it was the act of another and all reasonable steps were taken to avoid the offence. You must give notice of this to the prosecution at least 7 days before the first hearing.

The police have powers require the removal of a skip in contravention of the regulations and it is an offence to fail to comply with the request.

FAILURE TO COMPLY WITH TRAFFIC SIGNS

Most traffic signs are regulated by the Traffic Signs Regulations and General Directions 2002 SI 2002/3113 which prescribe the size, shape, colour and type as well as the positioning and location of a sign. If you are prosecuted in contravention of a sign it is worth checking the regulations and making sure that the sign you allegedly contravened complies if not the offence will not be enforceable.

There is a presumption that a sign is lawfully placed, so it will be up to you to rebut the presumption by showing that it is not lawfully placed and does not comply with the regulations. Using photographs of the sign together with the regulations will be very useful in presenting your argument.

Temporary Signs

Temporary signs are governed by the Traffic Signs (Temporary Obstructions) Regulations 1997 and covers regulations for the placing of cones, triangles, warning lamps, delineators and traffic pyramids for a temporary obstruction.

Non-compliance with a road traffic sign is prosecuted under S36 of the Road Traffic Act 1988. It requires a Notice of Intended Prosecution and covers signs listed in regulation 10. This also includes road markings such as double white lines and traffic lights.

Here are some examples:-

Sign height
750, 900, 1200

Sign	Dimensions
	300, 450, 600, 750, 900, 1200
	Sign height 600, 750, 900, 1200, 1500
	600, 750, 900, 1200
	450, 600, 750, 900, 1200
	450, 600, 750, 900, 1200
	450, 600, 750, 900, 1200

A single white line is not a traffic sign and therefore it is not an offence to cross it. However, it is an offence to cross a double white line or stop within the double white line system.

Traffic lights are also included within the regulations and are a road traffic sign. A vehicle must not cross the solid white line if the lights are on red, red/amber or amber unless the vehicle is so close that it cannot stop without crossing the white line.

Seat Belts

Seat belt regulations are found under the Road Vehicle (Construction and Use) Regulations 1986 for maintenance and fitting requirements and the Motor Vehicle (Wearing of Seat Belts) Regulations 1993 for wearing requirements. Breach of the latter is an offence in S14 Road Traffic Act 1988.

Any person over the age of 14 who contravenes the regulations commits an offence by virtue of S14(3) which states that whilst:-

- Driving a motor vehicle
- Riding in the front seat of a motor vehicle
- Riding in the rear seat

That person shall wear an adult seat belt.

The driver commits an offence if a person under 14 years of age does not wear a seat belt. The penalty for either offence is a level 2 fine of £500, band A.

Exceptions are:-

- Delivering or collecting goods on a journey not

exceeding 50 metres in a vehicle constructed/adapted for that purpose

- Fire/police powers
- Prisoner escorts
- Taxi driver carrying passengers
- Reversing
- Holder of a medical certificate
- No adult belt available.

Children

Front Seat Passenger

Under S15 (1) a driver must not without reasonable excuse drive a motor vehicle with a child under 14 years of age unless wearing a seat belt which conforms with the regulations. It is for the driver to establish that on a balance of probabilities that he had a reasonable excuse. It is difficult to see what would constitute a reasonable excuse.

Rear Seat Passenger

Under S15 (1) a driver must not without reasonable excuse drive a motor vehicle with a child under 14 years of age unless wearing a seat belt which conforms with the regulations. No child under the age of 12 or less than 150 cms in height should travel in the rear without a seat belt; even if there is one in the front not being used a driver must not drive that passenger car on a road without reasonable excuse. This means that if you have a seat belt in the front, a child should not sit in the front if there are no rear seat belts so the child should not travel in that car.

Exemptions:-

1. The child is over three years of age and a child restraint is not available front/back and the child is wearing an adult seat belt.
2. Where the child holds a medical certificate.
3. Where the child is under one year of age and is in a carry cot which is restrained by straps;
4. Where the child is disabled and is wearing a disabled person's belt.

Rear Seats Only

In a licensed taxi or licensed private hire care where the rear seats are separated from the driver where the vehicle is not a motor car nor passenger car. A child under the age of 3 must wear an approved restraint when travelling in either front/rear. A children aged 3 -11 yrs and under one and half metres in height must wear an appropriate child restraint when travelling in the front or rear, but may wear an adult seat belt in the front/rear if there is no restraint available.

A child aged 12-13years of age or younger or over one and half metres in height must wear a restraint appropriate for their height and weight or an adult seat belt.

A child over 14 years of age must wear an adult seat belt.

DEFECTIVE VEHICLE OFFENCES

There are a number of offences in this section and I shall deal with the various defective parts first.

Tyres

Tyres must comply with the regulations and it is an offence to use, cause or permit to be used on a road a vehicle subject to tyre approval on a road without a certificate of conformity: S63(1) of the Road Traffic Act 1988. The penalty is a level 4 fine £2,500.

S41A of the Road Traffic Act 1988

States that you will commit an offence if you fail to comply with the construction and use regulations as to brakes, steering gears or tyres.

The penalty is a level 5 fine of £5,000 for HGVs and PSVs or Level 4, £2,500 (Band C) for all others. 3 points or a discretionary disqualifications except if you can prove that you did not know and had no reasonable cause to suspect that the facts of the case were such that the offence would be committed.

The regulation in relation to tyres provides 8 different types of defect.

• The tyre is unsuitable having regard to the use to which the motor vehicle or trailer is being put or to the tyres or types of tyres fitted to its other wheels.

• The tyre is not so inflated as to make it fit for the use to which the motor vehicle or trailer is being put

• The tyre has a cut in excess of 25mm or 10 % of the section width of the tyre whichever is the greater, measured in any direction on the outside of the tyre and deep enough to reach the ply or cord.

• The tyre has any lump, bulge or tear caused by separation or partial failure of its structure

• The tyre has any of the ply or cord exposed

- The base of any groove which showed in the original tread patter of the tyre is not clearly visible

Either:-

i) the grooves of the tread pattern of the tyre do not have a depth of at least 1mm throughout a continuous band measuring at least three-quarters of the breadth of the tread patter of the tyre, did not extend beyond three-quarters of breadth of the tread, any groove which showed in the original tread patter does not have a depth of at least 1mm
or
ii) if the grooves of the original tread patter of the tyre did not extend beyond three-quarters of the breadth of the tread, any groove which showed in the original tread pattern does not have a depth of at least 1mm

- The tyre is not maintained in such condition as to be fit for the use to which the vehicle or trailer is being put or has a defect which might in any way cause damage to the surface of the road or damage to persons on or in the vehicle or to other persons using the road.

Tyre Tread Depths

Passenger motor cars other than cars constructed or adapted to carry more than eight passengers and light trailers	Min 1.6mm in continuous band over at least three-quarters of the breadth and around the entire circumference of the tyre.
Good Vehicles not exceeding 3,500 kg	Min 1.6mm in continuous band over at least three-quarters of the breadth and around the entire circumference of the tyre
All other applicable vehicles	Min 1mm in continuous band over at least three-quarters of breadth and around the entire circumference of the tyre.

Mixing Tyres

Regulation 26(1) pneumatic tyres of different types of structure shall not be fitted to the same axle of a wheeled vehicle.

A wheeled motor vehicle having only two axles each of which is equipped with one or two single wheels shall not be fitted with:-

a) a diagonal-ply tyre or bias-belted tyre on its rear axle if a radial-ply tyre is fitted on its front axle, or

b) a diagonal-ply tyre on its rear if a bias-belted tyre is fitted on the front axle.

This does not apply to a vehicle to an axle of which there are fitted wide tyres not specially constructed for use on engineering plant or to a vehicle which has a maximum speed not exceeding 30mph.

Pneumatic tyres fitted to either the steerable axles of a wheeled vehicle OR the driven axles of a wheeled vehicle, not being steerable axles, must be of the same type of structure.

Tyre Marking And Speed Rating

Reading a Tyre Sidewall

Every tyre sidewall shows information about the manufacturer, size, model etc.

Example: 205 40 R17 84W

• **205** - means the tyre has a nominal section width of 205 millimetres.

• **40** - is referred to as the aspect ratio and is the height of the tyre sidewall as a percentage of the nominal section width.

• **R** - means the tyre has a radial construction, the most commonly used of three different types of tyre construction: cross ply, radial and bias belted.

• **17** - means it fits a 17" diameter wheel.

• **84** - is the load index. This identifies the maximum load capacity of a tyre when driven at maximum speed. Overloading a tyre, by carrying more weight than it is designed to or running at a lower than specified pressure, can cause heat build up and blow outs. Load indexes for passenger cars usually range from 70 – 110.

The following table gives the maximum sustainable speed for tyres under normal use:

Tyre Speed Rating Symbol Table

Speed Symbol	Speed (Km/h)	Speed (mph)
L	120	75
M	130	81
N	140	87
P	150	93
Q	160	99
R	170	108
S	180	112
T	190	118
U	200	124
H	210	130
V	240	149
W	270	168
Y	300	186

Brakes

Regulation 18 is the most important regulation which you should know in relation to your vehicle's brakes. Every part of your braking system fitted to your vehicle and the means of operation must be in good and efficient working order and properly adjusted.

So one worn brake disc will be in contravention of reg 18 even if the whole of the braking system was efficient because ref 18 refers to every part and this means individual parts. The prosecution has to apply the usual criminal standard "beyond all reasonable doubt" but that does not mean that they must call an expert the fact that a police officer can push a car with the handbrake fully applied has been held to be sufficient evidence.

The offence is an absolute offence so claiming that you had done everything you could to ensure that the brakes were well maintained will not amount to a defence. If the brakes have a defect you will be guilty of the offence. Any argument about the maintenance and the fact that you may have relied on the garage may amount to special reasons. If you are concerned about such a charge you can get initial advice free from a specialist solicitor who for a fee would beable to present a special reasons argument for you.

The penalty is a level 5 fine £5,000/unlimited for offences committed after the 12th March 2015 for HGVs and PSVs, Level 4 fine £2,500 for others, 3 points or a discretionary disqualification.

Lights/fog lamps

Lights are governed by the Road Vehicles Lighting Regulations 1989, they cover the fitting and maintenance of lights and the use of lights:

- Headlamps
- Front and rear position lights (side lights)
- Stop lamps
- Reversing lamps
- Fog lamps
- Rear registration plate lights
- Other non-obligatory lights

It is an offence to cause or permit breach of these regulations.

S41 RTA 1988 Driving without lights is a level 4 fine £2,500 for HGV or PSV, and a level 3 £1,000 for other vehicles.

Other lighting offences including registration number plate is a level 4 fine £2,500 for HGV or PSV and level 3 £1,000 for other vehicles.

Fitting of Lamps

It is an offence to use, permit or cause on a road a vehicle specified in Schedule 1 that is not properly fitted with lamps and/or reflectors. It includes motor vehicles - 3+ wheels, solomotor bicycle, motorcycles, pedal cycles, pedestrian vehicles, the regulations control colour, flashing restrictions, warning lights.

Headlamps

Except for motorcycles, solo bicycles and certain 3 wheelers a vehicle must have two headlamps which must be properly matched and coloured white or yellow. They must be kept in good working order.

They must be lit during the hours of darkness or during seriously reduced visibility and must not cause undue dazzle or discomfort to other persons using the road or be lit whilst parked.

Fog Lamps

All vehicles first used on or after 1 April 1980 must have at least one rear fog lamp. If there is only one rear fog light fitted it must be fitted on the centre line of the vehicle or on the offside of the vehicle. Vehicles fitted with front fog lamps, which may be either white or yellow in colour, must ensure they comply with Schedule 6 as to fitting. It is an offence to switch on a front or rear fog lamp on a road other than in conditions of seriously reduced visibility. All fog lamps must be kept clean, in good working order and maintained so as not to cause undue dazzle or inconvenience.

Rear Registration Plate

It is an offence not to illuminate the rear index registration plate during the hours of darkness. A registration plate and the digits must comply in sizing, spacing, and must be made out of specified material. The size and style of each character is prescribed in Reg 14. Italic fonts and similar are prohibited.

Exhaust and Emissions

Every vehicle should be maintained so as not to emit any avoidable smoke or visible vapour.

There are precise levels of noxious emissions such as carbon monoxide. Reg 61.

It is an offence to use, cause or permit the use of a motor vehicle from which smoke, visible

Vapour or substance is emitted if it cause or may cause damage to any property or injury or

Danger to any person who is, maybe on the road.

Dangerous Condition

It is an offence under S40A to use, cause or permit another to use a motor vehicle to trailer on a road if:-

- the condition or the vehicle, accessories or equipment
- purpose for which it is used
- number of passengers or manner in which they are carried
- weight, position, distribution of load or way in which it is secured such that the use of the motor vehicle or trailer involves a danger of injury to any person. It carries a penalty of a level 5 fine £5,000/unlimited for offences committed after the 12th March 2015 if HGV/PSV or level 4 £2,500 (band B) for others.

Disqualification is obligatory if there has been a previous S40A within the previous three years otherwise it is discretionary or level 3 points.

Chapter Sixteen
Summons and Court

Most road traffic offences will be summonsed with the exception of drink driving and related offences, such as in charge or failing to supply a specimen of breath which will be charged and bailed at the police station or custody suite.

SUMMONS

A summons (postal requisition) is sent through the post with a form to indicate plea and also mitigation. Recently online pleas have been introduced, but you must be careful with these not to rush into the reply just because it is online and easy to do. It is the same as a guilty plea entered in a court room or written on a paper summons, so it is imperative that you consider your plea carefully and get legal advice before completing the form online. There are many firms such as Auriga Advocates who offer free initial advice and some will assist you in completing the form for a small fee. You do not usually have to attend court in answer to these, and the case can be dealt with in your absence, but you can attend if you wish. If the court are thinking about imposing a disqualification having heard the facts and seen previous convictions they will usually adjourn for you to attend.

CHARGE AND BAIL

A charge and bail is when you are charged at the police station and the custody sergeant will bail you to a court date. You will get a copy of the charge sheet and the bail notice. Bail means that you are ordered to attend court; failure to do so could result in a warrant for your arrest without good cause. It is imperative therefore that if you are ill, or unable to attend, that you notify the court immediately so that a warrant is not issued. If it is not a good reason, they may still issue a warrant.

UNSURE AS TO WHAT TO PLEAD?

There are a number of options you can take if you are unsure about your plea

1. The first and better option is to obtain advice as early as possible from a specialist solicitor. Most will give free initial advice and thereafter offer a range of services dependent on your circumstances and plea. You are not obliged to use these services but my advice would be to seriously consider doing so if you face serious penalties such as disqualification or imprisonment.

2. Leave your decision until the day of court. If you are charged with a non-imprisonable offence, you will not be eligible for the duty solicitor but some courts have triage advisors. Beware, these are prosecutors and often police officers. Whilst they will give you accurate advice as to the penalties, they should NOT be advising as to plea. This is unethical as they are prosecuting and cannot play both prosecution and defence. They do not advise you to seek independent advice, as they should. They will also have targets for dealing with matters at the first hearing, so it is in their interests to get you to plead. My advice is to get independent advice and not to rely on this service.

3. Use the duty solicitor at court? The duty solicitor is only allowed to represent you as a duty solicitor in the most serious offences which carry imprisonment. They will be able to represent you on an imprisonable offence, such as excess alcohol, but not on a not guilty plea and subsequent trial. They have numerous people to represent and very little time to prepare your case, often only allocating a matter of minutes. If you wish to plead not guilty they will speak to you in the hope that they can persuade you to hire their services privately, however I do not think this is the best environment to make hasty decisions and I have known many clients who have done this only to come to us at Auriga, having regretted their decision. I have dealt with the duty solicitor option in more detail in the charge and bail section of this chapter.

PLEADING GUILTY AFTER A SUMMONS

Pleading guilty by post

As explained earlier, this can be dealt with in your absence by you simply filling in the form that is attached to a summons. The form has a section for you to mitigate, which means that you should write information which you think will reduce your sentence.

Things to consider are:-

- good reason for driving
- lack of knowledge
- circumstances as to why you committed the offence
- personal circumstances
- financial circumstances if less than £400

It would be useful to have a look at the sentencing guidelines for your offence; these put the offence into sentencing bands depending on the circumstances of the offence, so you should use the lack of aggravating factors to put yourself in a lower band.

The fine bands A, B and C are an indication of the multiplier which they should apply to your net weekly income (after tax and National Insurance, not general outgoings).

Band A	25%-75% start point 50%
Band B	75%-125% start point 100%
Band C	125%-175% start point 150%

You should argue the fine level down the more mitigation you have. The sentencing guidelines are based on a person of previous good character who has been convicted after trial, therefore they should give a third credit on a guilty plea; they should reduce any penalty after consideration of the circumstances and which level you fall in by a third.

If you are on benefit or very low income similar to benefit, they should work on a weekly income of £120.

If your net weekly income is more than £400 at present it would be better not to provide details of your income, because if the court have no information they have to calculate any fine on an average weekly income of £400 (this is as at 2/2015 and may increase, so you should check the sentencing guidelines for the latest rates).

If you are uncomfortable writing any mitigation you can get a solicitor to write a letter of mitigation for you. If you use a specialist solicitor, they are used to mitigating motoring offences and can influence any sentence significantly. Such a letter is usually relatively low in cost and you should weigh up the saving in sentence and costs against the cost of the solicitor.

Obviously the higher the likely fine the most cost effective it can be to use a solicitor. However, you should also put a value on the endorsement, because points will usually increase your insurance premiums and could, with some offences, affect whether you are likely to be disqualified or not. If you are in the latter situation I think it would be good advice to secure the services of a solicitor to write a letter. A reasonable current rate in 2015 is between £175 and £250 depending on where you live. Some solicitors charge fixed rates whilst others have an hourly rate of between £150 and £200 per hour; if you instruct the latter, it could cost you considerably more. It is always better to instruct a solicitor who only deals with road traffic offences as they will usually have more experience and more time to dedicate to your case.

Attending Court to plead guilty

You can attend court to plead guilty if you wish rather than writing. It can influence your case significantly. Normally, the Magistrates are dealing with up to 100 or more of these cases in a day. Therefore they tend to get into a practice of absolute consistency. What I mean by that is that they listen to letters but routinely stick with the start point on the sentencing guidelines and issue the same sentence as the previous case with the same offence.

I have observed this in hundreds of road traffic courts over the years. Seldom do any letters of mitigation remind them that the starting point is a conviction after trial, so it is no surprise that they stick to the start point. By attending you can achieve two things:-

1. Clarify the start point and mitigate pointing out where you think the correct level of sentence is after mitigation. You can do this by making reference to the guidelines with each point of mitigation you raise.

2. You can demonstrate better the type of person you are and that the offence is out of character. The Magistrates deal with criminals in the main and do, as a matter of human nature, picture stereotypes. If you turn up in a suit, are polite and courteous to the court, you will to some extent change this picture, and as a result they will have more belief in your arguments and mitigation.

The procedure at court on a plea and mitigation (not special reasons or exceptional hardship, which is dealt with later in this chapter) is as follows.

Legal Advisor

The Legal Advisor who sits in front of the Magistrates and advises them on the law will identify you to the court, put the charge(s) to you and you can then enter your plea of guilty.

Usually if you are unrepresented, he/she will explain the procedure to you.

Prosecutor

The Prosecutor is the person responsible for charging and

presenting the case in court. In most road traffic cases this will be either a police officer or a civilian prosecutor. The Crown Prosecution Service only deals with not guilty pleas in minor road traffic cases or the more serious cases such as driving with excess alcohol or dangerous driving. The prosecutor will outline the case, usually by reading out the statement of facts which you will have had a copy of with the summons. They will also hand in any evidence of previous offences on your driving record.

Defendant

This is you, and after the prosecution have outlined the case you then have an opportunity to present your mitigation. You will usually be able to just outline this without having to give evidence on oath. This is usually only relevant when you are asking the Magistrates to reach a judgement on evidence which you wish to give to the court i.e. in special reason arguments or exceptional hardship.

Mitigation

You should follow a logical step by step approach to your mitigation, making reference to the sentencing guidelines. I would always follow the stages below:

1. I would always start with a brief introduction to the type of person you are and/or that the offence is out of character if that is the case.

2. Any factors which relate to the circumstances of the offence such as:

- Why you came to drive?
- Why you did not know you were insured?

- Why you committed the offence?
- Lack of knowledge that you were committing an offence?

These are examples and not an exhaustive list of possible factors which make your offending less serious and understandable, and thus lower your level of culpability and therefore reduce you penalty. You should list these factor prior to the hearing to use as a guide so that you do not forget anything.

At the end of this part of your mitigation, refer the magistrates to the guidelines suggesting where you come in the sentencing bands and why.

3. Personal circumstances which may even be a reason for the commission of the offence. This should include the type of person you are to try and show that the offence is out of character and the risk of re-offending is non-existent or very low. If you have evidence of being law abiding show it, i.e. producing insurance if you face a no insurance charge but on realisation you got insured immediately, or in the case of permit show that normally you are insured for the vehicle. Another example could be showing that you have taken the vehicle off the road and declared a SORN if prosecuted for no insurance because the vehicle was parked on the road but not being used.

4. Financial circumstances should be given if under £400; if not, do not discuss finance. You will have been given a means form to hand in but it is not obligatory and if you do not disclose your finance, then the court will work on an average of £400. You need to check this as it will change from year to year.

If you are of a very low income you may wish to argue that your income is so low that they should give you the rate of £120. It is advisable to complete the means form if this applies to you.

The means form is not a legally binding document. However, if the court make an official request, it is an offence not to supply details of your means. Due to this, if your income is significantly higher than £400 you may prefer to do a letter of mitigation omitting your means, as the court would not adjourn to request this information and would merely proceed on the £400. Alternatively you could instruct a solicitor to represent you in your absence and not provide details of means to him. Your representative is not permitted to disclose anything to the court that you have asked him not to.

Note that the above will not be an option if you are on bail, as you would have to attend.

Remember the midway point of the fine band is the court's starting point and your mitigation should bring it below that and the court should reduce by giving you credit for your prompt guilty plea.

You will need to hand in your driving licence if the offence carries points. You should make sure you take both parts to court and hand it in at the end of your mitigation along with any evidence you wish them to consider which you have referred to in your mitigation, such as character references or medical evidence.

After your mitigation the Magistrates will consider your representations and pass sentence. Your driving licence will be endorsed. If you still have a paper licence or the paper section of your licence this will not be returned to you. The online record will be updated with the details and you would have to access the information online. I would advise you to keep a copy of this record in a form that you have easy access to. If you are disqualified, your driving licence will be retained and you will have to apply for it at the end of your disqualification. You must make sure that you have your driving licence before you start driving again after your disqualification period is over.

Pleading guilty after being charged and bailed

If you are charged and bailed, you will have to attend court. Failure to do so without good reason will result in a warrant being issued. The reason has to be one that means you could not possibly have attend the court such as serious illness/accident it cannot be that you had an urgent meeting at work or similar.

Most motoring offences that are charged will be more serious, such as drink driving or failing to provide a specimen. Most carry a penalty of imprisonment.

Representing yourself

With these types of offences because of the serious nature of them I would not advise someone to represent themselves. If you do want to represent yourself seek some legal advice first.

If you are charged with more than one offence, you may be able to offer a plea one offence and ask the prosecutor to discontinue/withdraw the other offence(s). So getting initial advice is essential when you are charged with more than one offence.

Most specialist firm's offer detailed advice in these circumstances for between £75-100. Some can offer you written mitigation which you could read out in court, these would be the least expensive. However, none of these is as good as expert representation.

When you get to court you should check in and let the ushers know that you are representing yourself and ask where you can get the prosecution papers. You should get these and check with the prosecutor if you have previously agreed a basis of plea or pleas to certain offences and not others. The prosecution papers will consist of an outline of the circumstances of the offence and the prosecutor will usually read this out. If you disagree with any points, you should make a note of it. The papers will also include a list of any previous convictions, which if relevant will be handed into the court.

The usher at court will call you in when the court is ready to hear the case. This could be some time after your arrival so you must be patient and ready for a long wait. Once in court, the procedure is the same as outlined in the summons section.

However, although the stages are the same, the mitigation is much more important so you should have prepared thoroughly beforehand, emphasising any strong points in mitigation. Always ensure that you have the sentencing guidelines and pitch your mitigation in relation to the sentencing bands. If you have gained good advice beforehand you should be able to pitch the position of your offence in the most appropriate band.

Seeking representation at court

It is always advisable to get legal advice and sort out your legal representation before going to court, because this will enable more time and attention to be spent on your case. However, if you turn up to court without sorting representation you may be able to get some at court.

Imprisonable offences can be dealt with by the duty solicitor. When you arrive and check in, you will be asked if you want to see the duty solicitor.

Duty solicitors are paid by the Legal Aid Agency and are general criminal solicitors. They are not specialists and do not always provide the best advice. Remember it is important at this point that you take the correct steps, because it is only at this stage that the court must give you the full credit for a prompt plea; if you enter a not guilty plea at this point but decide to plead on the day of trial, the court do not have to give you any credit and therefore you would incur a much heavier penalty including court charges. (see Appendix 16) Duty solicitors work on a roster basis both at court and at the police station. The solicitor allocated to your court may have been on duty the night before, so may not have had much sleep. Usually there is only one per court but busier courts do have more. You may have to wait some time because the duty solicitor will have to see however many people who wish to get advice from him/her.

The duty solicitor will be able to give you advice as to your plea and will be able to represent you free of charge if you wish to plead guilty. If you wish to plead guilty he/she will obtain the prosecution papers and speak to the prosecution on your behalf. They will go through the papers with you and ask for information from you that they will use in mitigation. It is at this stage that you should provide any documentary evidence such as good character and your driving licence to hand into the court if required. As you will appreciate, he/she could be seeing quite a few people and going through the same procedure with them, so the mitigation may not be as detailed as you would like, but it is free.

Once in court your case will follow the same procedure but you will only be asked to confirm your identity and plea, the duty solicitor will make all other representations on your behalf.

You should not interrupt or speak directly to the magistrates unless they speak directly to you. If you want to make a point to the duty solicitor, either write a note to be passed to him or make a gesture such as raising your hand and saying excuse me so he knows you want to tell him something. Do not just shout out the problem; you may not do your case any good and will only annoy the duty solicitor and also the magistrates.

After sentence the duty solicitor should come and have a brief word with you to explain the sentence, but often they do not have time. You should in any event get a letter confirming what has gone on at court and providing you with post sentence advice.

Pleading guilty and pleading exceptional hardship

If you are likely to "tot up" the first step should be to try and persuade the magistrates to impose the lower number points if that enables you to avoid totting.

The court must impose the minimum period unless "having regard to all the circumstances there are no grounds for mitigating the normal consequences of a conviction". The court will not take into account any of the following grounds:

- any grounds alleged to make the offence less serious
- hardship other than exceptional hardship; and
- any circumstances taken into account by a court when the offender escaped disqualification or was disqualified for less than than the minimum period on a previous occasion within the three years preceding the current conviction, when he was liable to be disqualified under the totting up procedure.

The argument which can be considered is "exceptional hardship" although the court can take into account any other mitigating circumstances which do not fall into the exceptions above.

The hardship has to be exceptional and not just hardship, so loss of job, although that would seem exceptional to you, is not considered exceptional by the court. You must demonstrate the exceptional aspect of your hardship. Examples:-

• losing your job/financial impact on your family – eg loss of house.
• The impact that the disqualification would have on others- eg elderly relatives who depend on you driving or on your children getting to school because there is no public transport.
• The inability to continue voluntary work

You should get evidence of the impact such as letters from the charity you volunteer for, or from the people who depend on you driving them to places.

An important point to remember is that the emphasis should be on the impact on others and not yourself, because the court considers that you have brought the disqualification upon yourself, however other people who depend on you have not.

You cannot use the same argument again within three years, so if you have a really strong point which should amount to exceptional hardship but have others as well, it could be a good tactical move to just use that one argument so that if you "tot" again within three years you can use the other arguments.

If you wish to represent yourself, always be prepared. Make notes for yourself and get all the documentation that you need such as letters from charities/work/elderly relatives well before your court date. You be asked to give you arguments and present your evidence on oath and you could be cross examined by the prosecutor.

I would suggest that you at the very least get some advice from a specialist solicitor such as Auriga Advocates before you do this.

Solicitors will represent you by either writing a letter outlining the exceptional hardship or represent you in court. Expert representation is always better in these circumstances because they understand the legal arguments and what is more likely to influence the magistrates. A letter could only cost £200 and representation a lot more. Prices vary significantly between the specialist companies so it is worth checking. Remember paying more does not always mean that you are getting the best. Find out how experienced the representative will be; generally the more experience the better, read any testimonials and if you instruct a firm to represent you make sure that you know who is going to deal with your case in court. Some firms instruct barristers or agents or anyone who is available on the day, not necessarily the person you may have met. Most clients I represent want someone they have met and have formed a business relationship with and have gained some confidence in. It is always very disconcerting when someone turns up to represent you who you have never met before.

A duty solicitor could also do this as part of the plea and mitigation if the offence carries imprisonment.

Pleading Guilty and pleading Special Reasons against disqualification and endorsements

Most motoring offences carry a mandatory endorsement of points or a mandatory ban. You cannot plead mitigation to avoid these because the court has no option but to impose the points or disqualification. Mitigation will only work to reduce the number of points or the period of disqualification.

Special reason arguments are not based on personal circumstances but on the facts of the case. The rules involved are complicated and to establish whether you would have a valid reason you should seek expert legal advice which Auriga Advocates can provide.

Special reasons, if found, enable to the court to either not impose points or a ban at all or reduce the number of points or the period of the ban. It is an argument that can be used when you plead guilty or are found guilty of an offence and does not prevent you from arguing exceptional hardship if the court do not accept your special reason arguments.

Special reasons can be used for any offence but there is a strict criteria:

• The reason must be mitigating or extenuating circumstance;
• It must not amount to a defence;
• It must be directly connected to the commission of the offence, and
• The reason must be one that the court ought properly take into account when imposing punishment.

Examples of Special Reasons

1. Shortness of Distance
This is a common argument which is difficult to establish as the court has to consider the following:-
(i) distance driven
(ii) the manner in which it was driven
(iii) the state of the vehicle
(iv) whether the driver intended to go further
(v) the road and traffic conditions prevailing

(vi) whether there was a possibility of danger by coming into contact with other road users and pedestrians

(vii) what reason was the reason for the car being driven.

Therefore the fact that you may have only driven a few metres will not necessary suffice if you were on a busy road or car park, or the only reason you drove a short distance was that you were stopped by the police but had you not been stopped you would have driven further. Whether this argument applies to your case very much depends on the circumstances.

2. Laced drinks

This is the most common argument relating to drink driving offences, but is not as straight

forward as just proving that you had your drinks laced.

There are strict guidelines that the court must follow:-

(i) the defendant must be able to prove that his/her drinks were laced;

(ii) he/she did not know or suspect that his drink was "laced"; and

(iii) if his/her drink had not been laced the alcohol level in his/her blood would not have

exceeded the prescribed limit.

It is a difficult reason to prove and has very limited success. It often involves expert evidence. The law in this area is complicated and you need to seek legal advice before taking on this argument.

3. Emergency

It may be preferable to argue the defence of necessity/ duress of circumstance which would provide a complete defence rather than the special reasons argument of emergency, but the choice is not a simple one to make and very much depends on the circumstances surrounding your case. It is always difficult to justify committing an offence in these circumstances and you should always seek legal advice.

4. Insurance

If you are an employee then you would have a defence to driving without insurance if it was reasonable for you to assume your employer would have made insurance provisions. However, if you are genuinely misled about insurance it may amount to special reasons, but forgetting to renew your insurance or failing to pay the premiums or taking a friend's word for it without further investigation will not. So if you are asked to drive a car belonging to someone else, you should always check your insurance covers you or their insurance covers you; ask for sight of the documentation.

What are my options?

It is difficult to know what to do when charged with a motoring offence and often you may feel that you have some valid arguments to raise but do not know if they would amount to special reasons or a defence. This area of law is awash with case law and legal argument. I would not recommend that anyone try to represent themselves.

The procedure is straightforward.

At your first appearance you will enter a guilty plea, but state that you wish to raise a special reasons argument. The case will then be adjourned for a hearing with an allotted amount of time depending on which witnesses will be called. You will need to have considered the prosecution evidence to decide whether you wish to cross examine any of their witnesses or whether their statement can be agreed. Often they can be agreed, and the more statements that are read and fewer witnesses called, the lower the costs will be. It is difficult to know what to do in these circumstances and seeking early legal advice is vital. The procedure at the hearing is exactly the same as a trial (post).

NOT GUILTY PLEA AND TRIAL

If you wish to plead not guilty you should get some initial legal advice as early as possible and certainly before the first hearing. A specialist solicitor is always the best source of advice because all they do is road traffic cases, so they know much more than the average criminal solicitor. Some will give some fee basic advice and more detailed advice for about £75-£100. Some even offer a bespoke trial guide if you wish to represent yourself which can be a very useful, however these will cost £300 or more depending on the complexity of your case.

The duty solicitor can give you advice on plea and whether you will get legal aid to cover the costs of representation at court. However it is rare to get legal aid in road traffic cases. Most criminal legal aid firms will take on private paying clients so the duty will ask you if you want them to take on the case. My advice in this situation is that you take a card, but do not formally instruct them. Most criminal solicitors will charge you on the basis of an hourly rate of between £180 and £200 which can result in very expensive representation.

Most specialist solicitors will provide a fixed fee charge which means you will know exactly where you stand financially. Do some research before reaching your decision about legal representation; if you then wish to instruct the duty solicitor you saw, you can. You should remember that criminal legal aid firms rely on high turnover to make their money so less time and attention is dedicated to each case and many clients say that although they get accurate legal advice they do not feel supported. It is worth checking who would undertake your case at court, what experience they have and reading testimonials before reaching your decision.

Appendix 16 Prosecution costs

TRIAL GUIDE

A trial follows the following procedure: -

1. Legal Advisor	Will identify you and put the charge to you again asking you what you plead; if you wish to proceed to trial, you should plead not guilty
2. Prosecutor	Will outline the prosecution case which will be based on the evidence introduced by the police. He/she may refer to the law at this point. You or someone other than a witness should make notes as you will have to address this later.
3. Prosecutor	After the outline he/she will either call each prosecution witness and/or read some or all of the statements out depending on whether these have been agreed by the defence.
4. Prosecutor	At the end of their evidence having read all their statements and handed in exhibits they will close their case.

5. Defence	At this point you call your evidence i.e. yourself to give evidence on oath or affirm and your witnesses
6. Defence Witness Evidence	Each witness including yourself will go through the same procedure;

Examination in Chief You will give evidence according to your statement. Do not read from your statement although you should be allowed to refer to it if you wish, but ask the court first. It is better not to refer to it unless you have to. You will then be cross examined.

Your witness: will give evidence in answer to your questions based on her statement

Cross Examination: |

	Each witness will after giving their initial evidence will be cross examined by being asked questions by the prosecution. Re-examination : If any issues have arisen or you wish to re-inforce the evidence your or your witness have given you have the opportunity to do so after the cross examination.
7. Defence S 9 Evidence	This is defence evidence which is agreed with the prosecution and can be read to the court.
8. Defence Summary and Submission	This is when you have an opportunity to present your argument and make submissions as to why you are not guilty of the offence.

The above procedure is basically the same in every trial. Note that the prosecution do have an opportunity to answer your defence statement if they choose to do so; many do not.

Your Trial

PROSECUTION

The prosecution will outline their case based on the statements which should have already been disclosed to you.

The prosecutor may choose not to do an outline of the evidence and simply read the evidence out and present the exhibits or call the prosecution witnesses straight away. If there are any legal arguments, the prosecution will deal with them at this point.

Despite your urge to interrupt and correct the prosecutor with what you think is right, you **MUST NOT**. Your time to raise issue with the statements and anything that the prosecutor says comes later, and at a better time, because it can usually be the last thing the Magistrates hear.

It is important that notes are taken full of the evidence given so that you can refer to it in your defence submission.

DEFENCE

Now it will be your turn, but initially you should just present your evidence.

You

As you are both defence advocate and defendant – you will be asked if you wish to give evidence on oath, or affirm, which you should do. After giving the oath you should just give your evidence as per your statement. Stick to the facts, do not give personal opinion/feelings – stick to your evidence alone.

CROSS EXAMINATION

The prosecutor may ask you questions which will usually be to challenge your evidence and will highlight any discrepancies. My advice is to answer honestly. Do not get frustrated or say to the prosecutor things like, "Well, you were not there," or, "Well, what would you do?" Just answer the question, do not ask the prosecutor questions. If you do not know the answer say so, do not be tempted to give the answer you think they want. Avoid saying things like, "You are just trying to catch me out." If you do not understand a question, say so and ask them to repeat it.

RE EXAMINATION

In this part you can clarify and issues raised the prosecution and conclude by briefly running through the key parts of your evidence. This process will be followed by each witness but of course you will have to question your witnesses.

DEFENCE WITNESS

EXAMINATION IN CHIEF

Your witness must give evidence by you asking questions based on her statement. This can be difficult; you cannot ask leading questions so it is imperative that your witnesses know their statements well.

Example of leading question would be, "You saw John driving the car on the 1st October 2014 at 3.40pm didn't you?" A correct question would be, "What did you do at 3.40pm on the 1st October 2014?", "Who did you see at that time?", "What was he doing?"

You should go through their evidence and prepare questions to ask so each witness provides all the information you want to.

The types of questions will depend on the evidence the witness is giving.

CROSS EXAMINATION

This will be similar to the cross examination you have received.

RE-EXAMINATION

You should ask questions of your witnesses at this stage merely to clarify the issues raised by the prosecution in their cross examination

After all your live witnesses have given evidence, you can read out any statements that you have agreed. This can only be read if agreed with the prosecutor. You should send any statements you think may be agreed to the prosecution before the trial. They have 7 days in which to reply and agree or refuse the statement; if refused, you must call the witness to get their evidence in on the trial date. If there is no reply within 7 days, you can assume the statement is agreed. Make copies of any documents you will be handing in and statements to read. Four of each will ensure the prosecutor has one and each of the magistrates.

DEFENCE SUMMARY

This is probably the most important part of your case as this is your opportunity to put forward your arguments and submission. Very often it is the last thing the magistrates hear. This is where you can raise the issues with the prosecution evidence and also raise the differences in the case law with your case.

Take each stage at a time.

1. Prosecution evidence
Refer to your notes to point out discrepancies/inconsistences in the prosecution case if there are any.

Point out any elements of the offence that they have not proved.

2. Defence evidence
Point out the magistrates that you only have to prove your defence on a balance of probabilities, which is basically that it is more than likely to be true.

Emphasise the points in the defence case and points which are corroborated by more than one witness.

LEGAL ARGUMENTS

That just leaves your submissions and legal arguments. This should point out any elements of the offence you do not think are made out. You can refer to case law and definitions if you wish, but make sure you are accurate and have done your research on these points.

If The Court Do Not Find In Your Favour And Find You Guilty

If the court return having considered the evidence and find you guilty do not react. The prosecution will give the court a record of previous convictions and apply for their costs and any compensation.

Just provide the court with any mitigation as you would on a guilty plea (ante). Remember that you cannot ask for any credit because you have run a trial. The Magistrates have to read out their reasons in open court so you can use their findings to work out which level of sentencing applies in the guidelines.

You can make a submission of special reasons if:-

1. You have a mitigating or extenuating circumstance

2. Which is not a defence in law (if they find you guilty, they clearly have established they do not accept you have a defence).

3. It is directed to the commission of the offence, which it clearly is

4. It is one the court ought properly to take into consideration when imposing sentence.

The magistrates will probably already have heard the evidence so you would not have to go through it again, it will just be a case of running through the evidence and how that amounts to a special reason.

If you are "totting" you can also present your exceptional hardship case at this point.

Found Not Guilty

If you are found not guilty that will be the end of the matter. You may wish to ask for a defendant costs order, which will cover costs relating to the case itself and not things like loss of earnings etc.

Having read the trial procedure you are probably re-considering whether to represent yourself.

It will be a matter of economics as to whether you should or should not represent yourself. Cases which have low fines and no endorsement or few points which do not cause a problem may not justify the costs of representation. In this case get some advice and perhaps a bespoke trial guide which will be relatively inexpensive in comparison to trial representation costs. But remember that in any trial you must consider whether you can live with the worst case scenario. The greater the risk to your liberty, finance and licence, the more you should be considering paying for expert representation, because ultimately it will be a saving when you consider the cost of any penalty, the impact on insurance premiums and cost of not being able to drive or perhaps work.

YOUR BEST DEFENCE

Appendix 1
Fixed Penalty Offences

Offences under the Road Traffic Regulation Act 1984 (c.27)

RTRA section 5(1)	Using a vehicle in contravention of a traffic regulation order outside Greater London.
RTRA section 8(1)	Breach of traffic regulation order in Greater London.
RTRA section 11	Breach of experimental traffic order.
RTRA section 13	Breach of experimental traffic scheme regulations in Greater London.
RTRA section 16(1)	Using a vehicle in contravention of temporary prohibition or restriction of traffic in case of execution of works, etc.

RTRA section 17(4)	Wrongful use of special road.
RTRA section 18(3)	Using a vehicle in contravention of provision for one-way traffic on trunk road.
RTRA section 20(5)	Driving a vehicle in contravention of order prohibiting or restricting driving vehicles on certain classes of roads.
RTRA section 25(5)	Breach of pedestrian crossing regulations, except an RTRA section 29(3) offence in respect of a moving motor vehicle other than a contravention of regulations 23, 24, 25 and26 of the Zebra, Pelican and Puffin Pedestrian Crossings Regulations and General Directions 1997
RTRA section 29(3)	Using a vehicle in contravention of a street playground order

RTRA secti on35A(1)	Breach of an order regulating the use, etc., of a parking place provided by a local authority, but only where the offence is committed in relation to a parking place provided on a road
RTRA section 47(1)	Breach of a provision of a parking place designation order and other offences committed in relation to a parking place designated by such an order, except any offence of failing to pay an excess charge within the meaning of section 46
RTRA section 53(5)	Using vehicle in contravention of any provision of a parking place designation order having effect by virtue of section 53(1)(a) (inclusion of certain traffic regulation provisions).
RTRA section 53(6)	Breach of a provision of a parking place designation order having effect by virtue of section 53(1)(b) (use of any part of a road for parking without charge).

RTRA section 88(7)	Driving a motor vehicle in contravention of an order imposing a minimum speed limit under section 88(1)(b).
RTRA section 89(1)	Speeding offences under RTRA and other Acts.

RTA section 14	Breach of regulations requiring wearing of seat belts.
RTA section 15(2)	Breach of restriction on carrying children in the front of vehicles.
RTA section 15(4)	Breach of restriction on carrying children in the rear of vehicles.
RTA section 16	Breach of regulations relating to protective headgear for motor cycle drivers and passengers.
RTA section 19	Parking a heavy commercial vehicle on verge or footway.
RTA section 22	Leaving vehicle in dangerous position.
RTA section 23	Unlawful carrying of passengers on motor cycles.
RTA section 24	Carrying more than one person on a pedal cycle.
RTA section 34	Driving mechanically propelled vehicle elsewhere than on a road.

RTA section 35	Failure to comply with traffic directions.
RTA section 36	Failure to comply with traffic signs.
RTA section 40A	Using vehicle in dangerous condition etc.
RTA section 41A	Breach of requirement as to brakes, steering-gear or tyres.
RTA section 41B	Breach of requirement as to weight: goods and passenger vehicles.
RTA sec tion 41D	Breach of requirement as to mobile phone use and proper control
RTA section 42	Breach of other construction and use requirements
RTA section 87(1)	Driving vehicle otherwise than in accordance with requisite licence.
RTA section 163	Failure to stop vehicle on being so required by constable
RTA section 3	Driving without Due care and attention or inconsiderate driving (July 2013)

Section 33 of the Vehicle Excise and Registration Act 1994.	Using or keeping a vehicle on a public road without vehicle licence, trade licence or nil licence being exhibited in manner prescribed by regulations.
Section 42 of that Act.	Driving or keeping a vehicle without required registration mark
Section 43 of that Act.	Driving or keeping a vehicle with registration mark obscured etc.
Section 59 of that Act	Failure to fix a prescribed registration mark to a vehicle in accordance with regulations made under section 23(4)(a) of that Act.

Appendix 2
Sentencing Guidelines to Driving Without Insurance

No Insurance	Road Traffic Act 1988, s.143

Triable only summarily:
Maximum: Level 5 fine

Must endorse and may disqualify. If no disqualification, impose 6-8 points - see notes below.

Offence seriousness (culpability and harm)
A. Identify the appropriate starting point

Starting points based on first time offender pleading not guilty

Examples of nature of activity	Starting Point	Range
Using a motor vehicle on a road or other public place without insurance	Band C fine	Band C fine 6 points - 12 months disqualification

Offence seriousness (culpability and harm)
B. Consider the effect of aggravating and mitigating factors (other than those within examples above)

Common aggravating and mitigating factors are identified in the pullout card - the following may be particularly relevant but **these lists are not exhaustive**

Factors indicating higher culpability	Factors indicating lower culpability
1. Never passed Test 2. Gave false details 3. Driving LGV, HGV, PSV 4. Driving for hire or reward 5. Evidence of sustained uninsured use **Factors indicating greater degree of harm** 1. Involved in accident 2. Accident resulting in injury	1. Responsibility for providing insurance rests with another 2. Genuine misunderstanding 3. Recent failure to transfer vehicle details where insurance was in existence 4. Vehicle not being driven

Appendix 3
Driving Licence Codes
and Penalty Points

**EACH ENDORSEMENT HAS A SPECIAL CODE
AND IS GIVEN 'PENALTY POINTS' ON A SCALE
FROM 1 TO 11. YOU GET MORE POINTS FOR
MORE SERIOUS OFFENCES.**

The table shows the offence codes that can be put on
your driving licence. It also shows how many penalty points
you can get for them. Some offences may also involve a
disqualification.

Offence codes and penalty points must stay on your
driving licence for 4 or 11 years depending on the offence.

Offence Code	Offence	Penalty Points	Number of Years on Licence
AC20	Failing to give particulars or report an accident within 24hrs	5-10	4
AC30	Undefined accident offences	4-9	4
BA10	Driving while disqualified by order of court	6	4
BA30	Attempting to drive while disqualified by order of court	6	4
CD10	Driving without due care and attention	3-9	4
CD20	Driving without reasonable consideration for other road users	3-9	4

CD30	Driving without due care and attention or without reasonable consideration for other road users	3-9	4
CD40	Causing death through careless driving when unfit through drink	3-11	11
CD50	Causing death by careless driving when unfit through drug	3-11	11
CD60	Causing death by careless driving when unfit through drug	3-11	11
CD70	Causing death by careless driving when failing to supply a specimen for alcohol analysis	3-11	11

CD80	Causing death by careless, or inconsiderate driving	3-11	4
CD90	Causing death by driving without insurance/ driving licence	3-11	4
CU10	Using a vehicle with defective breaks	3	4
CU20	Causing or likely to cause danger by reason of use of unsuitable vehicle or using a vehicle with parts or accessories (excluding brakes, steering or tyres) in a dangerous condition	3	4
CU30	Using a vehicle with defective tyres	3	4

CU40	Using a vehicle with defective steering	3	4
CU50	Causing or likely to cause danger by reason of load or passengers	3	4
CU80/ CU84	Using a mobile phone or hand held device/not being in proper control	3-6	4
DD10	Causing serious injury by dangerous driving	3-11	4
DD40	Dangerous driving	3-11	4
DD60	Manslaughter or culpable homicide while driving a vehicle	3-11	4
DD80	Causing death by dangerous driving	3-11	4

DD90	Furious driving	3-9	4
DR10	Driving by attempting to drive with alcohol level above 1	3-11	11
DR20	Driving or attempting to drive with alcohol level above 1	3-11	11
DR30	Driving or attempting to drive then failing to supply a specimen for analysis	3-11	11
DR31	Driving or attempting to drive then refusing to give permission for analysis of a blood sample that was taken without consent due to incapacity	3-11	11

DR40	In charge of a vehicle while alcohol level above limit	10	4
DR50	In charge of vehicle while unfit through drink	10	4
DR60	Failure to provide a specimen for analysis in circumstances other than driving or attempting to drive	10	4
DR61	Refusing to give persmission for analysis of a blood sample that was taken without consent due to incapacity in circumstances other than driving or attempting to drive	10	11

DR70	Failing to provide specimen for breath test	4	4
DR80	Driving or attempting to drive when unfit through drugs	3-11	11
DR90	In charge of a vehicle when unfit through drugs	10	4
IN10	Using a vehicle uninsured against third party risks	6-8	4
LC20	Driving otherwise than in accordance with a licence	3-6	4
L30	Driving after making a false declaration about fitness when applying for a licence	3-6	4

LC40	Driving a vehicle having failed to notify a disability	3-6	4
LC50	Driving after a licence has been revoked or refused on medical grounds	3-6	4
MS10	Leaving a vehicle in a dangerous position	3	4
MS20	Unlawful pillion riding	3	4
MS50	Motor racing on the highway	3-11	4
MS60	Motor racing on the highway	3	4
MS60	Motor racing on the highway	3	4
MS70	Driving with uncorrected defective eyesight	3	4

MS80	Refusing to submit to an eyesight test	3	4
MS90	Failure to give information as to identity of driver, etc	6	4
MW10	Contravention of special roads regulations (excluding speed limits)	3	4
PC10	Undefined contravention of pedestrian crossing regulations	3	4
PC20	Undefined contravention of pedestrian crossing regulations	3	4
PC30	Contravention of pedestrian crossing regulations with stationary vehicle	3	4

SP10	Contravention of pedestrian crossing regulations with stationary vehicle	3-6	4
SP20	Exceeding speed limit for type of vehicle (excluding goods or passenger vehicles)	3-6	4
SP30	Exceeding statutory speed limit on a public road	3-6	4
SP40	Exceeding statutory speed limit on a public road	3-6	4
SP50	Exceeding speed limit on a motorway	3-6	4
TS10	Failing to comply with traffic light signals	3	4

TS20	Failing to comply with double white lines	3	4
TS40	Failing to comply with direction of a constable/ warden	3	4
TS50	Failing to comply with traffic sign (excluding 'stop' signs, traffic lights or double white lines)	3	4
TS60	Failing to comply with a school crossing patrol sign	3	4
TS70	Undefined failure to comply with a traffic direction sign	3	4
TT90	Disqualification under "totting up"	12 points or more within 3 yrs driver can be disqualified	4

UT50	Aggravated taking of a vehicle	3-11	4
MR09 (MR offences relate to offences in Northern Ireland, Isle of Man or Republic of Ireland disqualification is valid in GB)	Reckless or dangerous driving (whether or not resulting in death, injury or serious risk)		
MR19	Wilful failure to carry out the obligation placed on driver after being involved in a road accident (hit or run)		

MR29	Driving a vehicle while under the influence of alcohol or other substance affecting or diminishing the mental and physical abilities of a driver		
MR39	Driving a vehicle faster than the permitted speed		
MR49	Driving a vehicle whilst disqualified		
MR59	Other conduct constituting an offence for which a driving disqualification has been imposed by the State of Offence		

Aiding, abetting, counselling or procuring offences

For these offences, the codes are similar but with the number 0 on the code changed to 2.

For example code LC20 (driving otherwise than in accordance with a licence) becomes code LC22 if you have helped someone to do this.

Causing or permitting offences

For these offences, the codes are similar, but with the number 0 on the code changed to 4.

For examples LC20 (driving other than in accordance with a licence) becomes LC24 if you have caused or permitted someone to do this.

Inciting offences

For these offences, the codes are similar, but with the number 0 on the code changed to 6.

For example DD40 (dangerous driving) becomes DD46 on your licence if you've incited someone to do this.

Appendix 4

PART 1

(1) Category or Sub-Category	(2) Classes of Vehicle Included	(3) Additional Categories and Sub-Categories
A	Motor bicycles	B1, K and P
A1	A sub-category of category A comprising learner motor bicycles.	P

B	Motor vehicles, other than vehicles included in category A, F, K or P, having a maximum authorised mass not exceeding 3.5 tonnes and not more than eight seats in addition to the driver's seat, including: (i) a combination of any such vehicle and a trailer where the trailer has a maximum authorised mass not exceeding 750 kilogrammes, and (ii) a combination of any such vehicle and a trailer where the maximum authorised mass of the combination does not exceed 3.5 tonnes and the maximum authorised mass of the trailer does not exceed the unladen weight of the tractor vehicle.	F, K and P

B1	A sub-category of category B comprising motor vehicles having three or four wheels and an unladen weight not exceeding 550 kilograms.	K and P
B+E	Combinations of a motor vehicle and trailer where the tractor vehicle is in category B but the combination does not fall within that category.	None
C	Motor vehicles having a maximum authorised mass exceeding 3.5 tonnes, other than vehicles falling within category D, F, G or H, including any such vehicle drawing a trailer having a maximum authorised mass not exceeding 750 kilograms.	None

C1	A sub-category of category C comprising motor vehicles having a maximum authorised mass exceeding 3.5 tonnes but not exceeding 7.5 tonnes, including any such vehicle drawing a trailer having a maximum authorised mass not exceeding 750 kilograms.	None
D	Motor vehicles constructed or adapted for the carriage of passengers having more than eight seats in addition to the driver's seat, including any such vehicle drawing a trailer having a maximum authorised mass not exceeding 750 kilograms.	None
D1	A sub-category of category D comprising motor vehicles having more than eight but not more than 16 seats in addition to the driver's seat and including any such vehicle drawing a trailer with a maximum authorised mass not exceeding 750 kilograms.	None

C+E	Combinations of a motor vehicle and trailer where the tractor vehicle is in category C but the combination does not fall within that category.	B+E
C1+ E	A sub-category of category C+E comprising combinations of a motor vehicle and trailer where: (a) the tractor vehicle is in sub-category C1, (b) the maximum authorised mass of the trailer exceeds 750 kilograms but not the unladen weight of the tractor vehicle, and (c) the maximum authorised mass of the combination does not exceed 12 tonnes.	B+E
D+E	Combinations of a motor vehicle and trailer where the tractor vehicle is in category D but the combination does not fall within that category.	B+E

D1+E	A sub-category of category D+E comprising combinations of a motor vehicle and trailer where: (a) the tractor vehicle is in sub-category D1, (b) the maximum authorised mass of the trailer exceeds 750 kilograms but not the unladen weight of the tractor vehicle, (c) the maximum authorised mass of the combination does not exceed 12 tonnes, and (d) the trailer is not used for the carriage of passengers.	B+E
F	Agricultural or forestry tractors, including any such vehicle drawing a trailer but excluding any motor vehicle included in category H.	K
G	Road rollers	None
H	Track-laying vehicles steered by their tracks.	None

K	Mowing machines which do not fall within category A and vehicles controlled by a pedestrian.	None
P	Mopeds	None

PART 2

(1) Category or Sub-Category	(2) Classes of Vehicle Included	(3) Additional Categories and Sub-Categories
C1+E (8.25 tonnes)	A sub-category of category C+E comprising combinations of a motor vehicle and trailer in sub-category C1+E, the maximum authorised mass of which does not exceed 8.25 tonnes.	None

D1 (not for hire or reward)	A sub-category of category D comprising motor vehicles in sub-category D1 driven otherwise than for hire or reward.	None
D1+E (not for hire or reward)	A sub-category of category D+E comprising motor vehicles in sub-category D1+E driven otherwise than for hire or reward.	None
L	Motor vehicles propelled by electrical power.	None

Eligibility to apply for provisional licence

11. (1) Subject to the following provisions of this regulation, an applicant for a provisional licence authorising the driving of motor vehicles of a class included in a category or sub-category specified in column (1) of the table at the end of this regulation must hold a relevant full licence authorising the driving of motor vehicles of a class included in the category or sub-category specified in column (2) of the table in relation to the first category.

(2) Paragraph (1) shall not apply in the case of an applicant who is a full-time member of the armed forces of the Crown.

(3) For the purposes of paragraph (1), a licence authorising the driving only of vehicles in sub-categories D1 (not for hire or reward), D1+E (not for hire or reward) and C1+E (8.25 tonnes) shall not be treated as a licence authorising the driving of motor vehicles of a class included in sub-categories D1, D1+E and C1+E.

(4) In this regulation, "relevant full licence" means a full licence granted under Part III of the Traffic Act, a full Northern Ireland licence, a full British external licence (other than a licence which is to be disregarded for the purposes of section 89(1)(d) of the Traffic Act by virtue of section 89(2)(c) of that Act(1)), a full British Forces licence, an exchangeable licence or a Community licence.

(1) Category or sub-category of licence applied for	(2) Category/sub-category of full licence required
B+E	B
C	B
C1	B
D	B
D1	B
C1+E	C1
C+E	C
D1+E	D1

G	B
H	B

Full licences not carrying provisional entitlement

19. (1) The application of sections 98(2) and 99A(5) of the Traffic Act is limited or excluded in accordance with the following paragraphs.

(2) Subject to paragraphs (3), (4), (5), (6), (11) and (12), the holder of a full licence which authorises the driving of motor vehicles of a class included in a category or sub-category specified in column (1) of the table at the end of this regulation may drive motor vehicles—

(a)of other classes included in that category or sub-category, and

(b)of a class included in each category or sub-category specified, in relation to that category or sub-category, in column (2) of the table,

as if he were authorised by a provisional licence to do so.

(3) Section 98(2) shall not apply to a full licence if it authorises the driving only of motor vehicles adapted on account of a disability, whether pursuant to an application in that behalf made by the holder of the licence or pursuant to a notice served under section 92(5)(b) of the Traffic Act.

(4) In the case of a full licence which authorises the driving of a class of standard motor bicycles, other than bicycles included in sub-category A1, section 98(2) shall not apply so as to authorise the driving of a large motor bicycle by a person under the age of 21 before the expiration of the standard access period.

(5) In the case of a full licence which authorises the driving of motor bicycles of a class included in sub-category A1 section 98(2) shall not apply so as to authorise the driving of a large motor bicycle by a person under the age of 21.

(6) In the case of a full licence which authorises the driving of a class of vehicles included in category C or C+E, paragraph (2) applies subject to the provisions of regulation 54.

(7) Subject to paragraphs (8), (9), (10), (11) and (12), the holder of a Community licence to whom section 99A(5) of the Traffic Act applies and who is authorised to drive in Great Britain motor vehicles of a class included in a category or sub-category specified in column (1) of the Table at the end of this regulation may drive motor vehicles—

(a) of other classes included in that category or sub-category, and

(b) of a class included in each category or sub-category specified, in relation to that category or sub-category, in column (2) of the Table,as if he were authorised by a provisional licence to do so.

(8) Section 99A(5) shall not apply to a Community licence if it authorises the driving only of motor vehicles adapted on account of a disability.

(9) In the case of a Community licence which authorises the driving of a class of standard motor bicycle other than bicycles included in sub-category A1, section 99A(5) shall not apply so as to authorise the driving of a large motor bicycle by a person under the age of 21 before the expiration of the period of two years commencing on the date when that person passed a test for a licence authorising the driving of that class of standard motor bicycle (and in calculating the expiration of that period, any period during which that person has been disqualified for holding or obtaining a licence shall be disregarded).

(10) In the case of a Community licence which authorises the driving only of motor bicycles of a class included in sub-category A1 section 98(2) shall not apply so as to authorise the driving of a large motor bicycle by a person under the age of 21.

(11) Except to the extent provided in paragraph (12), section 98(2) shall not apply to a full licence, and section 99A(5) shall not apply to a Community licence, in so far as it authorises its holder to drive motor vehicles of any class included in category B+E, C+E, D+E or K or in sub-category B1 (invalid carriages), C1 or D1 (not for hire or reward).

(12) A person—

(a)who holds a full licence authorising the driving only of those classes of vehicle included in a category or sub-category specified in paragraph (11) which have automatic transmission (and are not otherwise adapted on account of a disability), or

(b)who holds a Community licence, to whom section 99A(5) of the Traffic Act applies and who is authorised to drive in Great Britain only those classes of vehicle included in a category or sub-category specified in paragraph (11) which have automatic transmission (and are not otherwise adapted on account of a disability),may drive motor vehicles of all other classes included in that category or sub-category which have manual transmission as if he were authorised by a provisional licence to do so.

(1) Full Licence Held	(2) Provisional Entitlement Included
A1	A, B, F and K
A	B and F
B1	A, B and F
B	A, B+E, G and H
C	C1+E, C+E
D1	D1+E
D	D1+E, D+E
F	B and P
G	H
H	G
P	A, B, F and K

Appendix 5
Sentencing Guidelines for Speeding Offences

Note for offence committed on/after 12th March 2015
level 5 fines are unlimited

Speeding	Road Traffic Regulation Act 1984, s.89 (10)

Triable only summarily:

Maximum: Level 3 fine (level 4 if motorway)

Must endorse and may disqualify. If no disqualification, impose 3-6 points

Offence seriousness (culpability and harm)
A. Identify the appropriate starting point

Starting points based on first time offender pleading not guilty

Speed Limit		Recorded Speed (mph)	
20	21-30	31-40	41-50

30	31-40	41-50	51-60
40	41-55	56-65	66-75
50	51-65	66-75	76-85
60	61-80	81-90	91-100
70	71-90	91-100	101-110
Starting Point	**Band A fine**	**Band B fine**	**Band C fine**
Range	**Band A fine**	**Band B fine**	**Band C fine**
Points/ disqualification	**3 points**	**4-6 points OR disqualify 7 - 28 days**	**Disqualify 7 - 56 days OR 6 points**

Offence seriousness (culpability and harm)
B. Consider the effect of aggravating and mitigating factors (other than those within examples above)

Common aggravating and mitigating factors are identified in the pullout card - the following may be particularly relevant but **these lists are not exhaustive**

Factors indicating higher culpability	Factors indicating lower culpability
1. Poor road or weather conditions 2. Driving LGV, HGV, PSV etc 3. Towing caravan/trailer 4. Carrying passengers or heavy load 5. Driving for hire or reward 6. Evidence of unacceptable standard of driving over and above speed	1. Genuine emergency established
Factors indicating greater degree of harm	
1. Location e.g near school 2. High level of traffic or pedestrians in the vicinity	

Appendix 6
Sentencing Guidelines for Dangerous Driving

Note for offence committed on/after 12th March 2015
level 5 fines are unlimited

Dangerous Driving	Road Traffic Act 1988, s.2

Triable either way:

Maximum when tried summarily: Level 5 fine and/or 6 months

Maximum when tried on indictment: 2 years

• Must endorse and disqualify for at least 12 months. Must order extended re-test

• Must disqualify for **at least** 2 years if offender has had two or more disqualifications for periods of 56 days or more in preceding 3 years

If there is a delay in sentencing after conviction, consider interim disqualification

Offence seriousness (culpability and harm)
A. Identify the appropriate starting point

Starting points based on first time offender pleading not guilty

Examples of nature of activity	Starting Point	Range
Single incident where little or no damage or risk of personal injury	Medium level community order	Low level community order to high level

Disqualify 12-15 months |
| Incident(s) involving excessive speed or showing off, especially on busy roads or in built-up area; OR Single incident where little or no damage or risk of personal injury but offender was disqualified driver | 12 weeks custody | High level community order to 26 weeks custody

Disqualify 15-24 months |
| Prolonged bad driving involving deliberate disregard for safety of others; OR Incident(s) involving excessive speed or showing off, specially on busy roads or in built-up area, by disqualified driver; OR Driving as described in box above while being pursued by police | Crown Court | Crown Court |

Offence seriousness (culpability and harm)

B. Consider the effect of aggravating and mitigating factors (other than those within examples above)

Common aggravating and mitigating factors are identified in the pullout card - the following may be particularly relevant but **these lists are not exhaustive**

Factors indicating higher culpability	Factors indicating lower culpability
1. Disregarding warnings of others 2. Evidence of alcohol or drugs 3. Carrying out other tasks while driving 4. Carrying passengers or heavy load 5. Tiredness 6. Agressive driving, such as driving much too close to vehicle in front, racing, inappropriate attempts to overtake, or cutting in after overtaking 7. Driving when knowingly suffering from a medial condition which significantly impairs the offender's driving skills 8. Driving a poorly maintained or dangerously loaded vehicle, especially where motivated by commercial concerns **Factors indicating greater degree of harm** 1. Injury to others 2. Damage to other vehicles or property	1. Genuine emergency 2. Speed not excessive 3. Offence due to inexperience rather than irresponsibility of driver

Appendix 7
Sentencing Guidelines for Death by Careless and Inconsiderate Driving

Note for offence committed on/after 12th March 2015
level 5 fines are unlimited

Causing death by careless or inconsiderate driving	Road Traffic Act 1988, s.2B

Triable either way:

Maximum when tried summarily: Level 5 fine and/or 6 months

Maximum when tried on indictment: 5 years

Offence seriousness (culpability and harm)
A. Identify the appropriate starting point

Starting points based on first time offender pleading not guilty

Examples of nature of activity	Starting Point	Range
Careless or inconsiderate driving arising from momentary inattention with no aggravating facors	Medium level community order	Low level community order to high level community order
Other cases of careless or inconsiderate driving	Crown Court	High level community order to Crown Court
Careless or inconsiderate driving failing not far short of dangerous driving	Crown Court	Crown Court

Offence seriousness (culpability and harm)

B. Consider the effect of aggravating and mitigating factors (other than those within examples above)

Common aggravating and mitigating factors are identified in the pullout card - the following may be particularly relevant but **these lists are not exhaustive**

Factors indicating higher culpability	Factors indicating lower culpability
1. Other offences committed at the same time, such as driving	1. Offender seriously injured in collision

other than in accordance with the terms of a valid licence; driving while disqualified; driving without insurance; taking a vehicle without consent; driving a stolen vehicle

2. Previous convictions for motoring offences, particularly offences that involve bad driving

3. Irresponsible behavious, such as failing to stop or falsely claiming that one of the victims was responsible for the collision

Factors indicating greater degree of harm

1. More than one person was killed as a result of the offence

2. Serious injury to one or more persons in addition to the death(s)

2. The victim was a close friend or relative

3. The actions of the victim or a third party contributed to the commission of the offence

4. The offender's lack of driving experience contributed significantly to the likelihood of a collision occuring and/or death resulting

5. The driving was in response to a proven and genuine emergency falling short of a defence

Appendix 8
Sentencing Guidelines for Driving Without Care and Attention

Note for offence committed on/after 12th March 2015 level 5 fines are unlimited

Careless driving (drive without due care and attention)	Road Traffic Act 1988, s.3

Triable only summarily:
Maximum: Level 5 fine

Must endorse and may disqualify. If no disqualification, impose 3-9 points

Offence seriousness (culpability and harm)
A. Identify the appropriate starting point

Starting points based on first time offender pleading not guilty

Examples of nature of activity	Starting Point	Range
Momentary lapse of concentration or misjudgement at low speed	Band A fine	Band A fine 3-4 points
Loss of controle due to speed, mishandling or insufficient attention to road conditions, or carelessly turning right across on-coming traffic	Band B fine	Band B fine 5-6 points
Overtaking manoeuvre at speed resulting in collision of vehicles, or driving bordering on the dangerous	Band C fine	Band C fine Consider disqualification OR 7-9 points

Offence seriousness (culpability and harm)

B. Consider the effect of aggravating and mitigating factors (other than those within examples above)

Common aggravating and mitigating factors are identified in the pullout card - the following may be particularly relevant but **these lists are not exhaustive**

Factors indicating higher culpability	Factors indicating lower culpability
1. Excessive speed 2. Carrying out other tasks while driving 3. Carrying passengers or heavy load 4. Tiredness	1. Minor risk 2. Inexperience of driver 3. Sudden change in road or weather conditions

Factors indicating greater degree of harm	
1. Injury to others 2. Damage to other vehicles or property 3. High level or traffic or pedestrians in vicinity 4. Location e.g. near school when children are likely to be present	

Form a preliminary view of the appropriate sentence, then consider offender mitigation

Common factors are identified in the pullout card

Consider a reduction for guilty plea

Consider ordering disqualification until appropriate driving test passed
Consider ancillary orders, including compensation

Decide sentence
Give reasons

Appendix 9
Sentencing for Failing to Stop/Report

Note for offence committed on/after 12th March 2015
level 5 fines are unlimited

Fail to stop/report road accident	Road Traffic Act 1988, s.170(4)

Triable only summarily:
Maximum: Level 5 fine and/or 6 months

Must endorse and may disqualify. If no disqualification, impose 5-10 points

Offence seriousness (culpability and harm)
A. Identify the appropriate starting point

Starting points based on first time offender pleading not guilty

Examples of nature of activity	Starting Point	Range
Minor damage/injury or stopped at scene but failed to exchange particulars or report	Band B fine	Band B fine 5-6 points
Moderate damage/injury or failed to stop and failed to report	Band C fine	Band C fine 7-8 points Consider disqualification
Serious damage/injury and/or evidence of bad driving	High level community order	Band C fine to 26 weeks custody Disqualify 6-12 months OR 9-10 points

Offence seriousness (culpability and harm)

B. Consider the effect of aggravating and mitigating factors (other than those within examples above)

Common aggravating and mitigating factors are identified in the pullout card - the following may be particularly relevant but **these lists are not exhaustive**

Factors indicating higher culpability	Factors indicating lower culpability
1. Evidence of drink or drugs/ evasion of test	1. Believed identity known 2. Genuine fear of retribution

2. Knowledge/suspicion that personal injury caused (where not an element of the offence) 3. Leaving injured party at scene 4. Giving false details	3. Subsequently reported

Appendix 10
Sentencing Guidelines for In Charge Whilst Unfit Through Drink or Drugs

Unfit through drink or drugs (drive/attempt to drive)	Road Traffic Act 1988, s.4(1)

Triable only summarily:
Maximum: Level 5 fine and/or 6 months

• Must endorse and disqualify for at least 12 months
• Must disqualify for **at least** 2 years if offender has had two or more disqualificationsfor periods of 56 days or more in preceeding 3 years
• Must disqualify for **at least** 3 years if offender has been convicted of a relevant offence in preceeding 10 years

If there is a delay in sentencing after conviction, consider interim disqualification

Note: the final column below provides guidance regarding the length of disqualification that may be appropriate in cases to which the 3 year minimum applies. The period to be imposed in any individual case will depend on an assessment of all the relevant circumstances, including the length of time since the earlier ban was imposed and the gravity of the current offence.

Offence seriousness (culpability and harm)
A. Identify the appropriate starting point

Starting points based on first time offender pleading not guilty

Examples of nature of activity	Starting Point	Range	Dis-qualification	Dis. 2nd offence in 10 years
Evidence of moderate level of impairment and no aggravating factors	Band C fine	Band C fine	12-16 months	36 to 40 months
Evidence of moderate level of impairement and presence of one or more aggravating factors listed below	Band C fine	Band C fine	17-22 months	36 to 46 months

Evidence of high level of impairment and no aggravating factors	Medium level comm. order	Low level comm. order to high level comm. order	23-28 months	36 to 52 months
Evidence of high level of impairment and presence of one or more aggravating factors listed below	12 weeks custody	High level comm. order to 26 weeks custody	29-36 months	36 to 50 months

Offence seriousness (culpability and harm)

B. Consider the effect of aggravating and mitigating factors (other than those within examples above)

Common aggravating and mitigating factors are identified in the pullout card - the following may be particularly relevant but **these lists are not exhaustive**

Factors indicating higher culpability	Factors indicating lower culpability
1. LGV, HGV, PSV, etc	1. Genuine emergency established*
2. Poor road or weather conditions	2. Spiked drinks*
3. Carrying passengers	3. Very short distance driven*

4. Driving for hire or reward 5. Evidenceof unacceptable standard of driving **Factors indicating greater degree of harm:** 1. Involved in accident 2. Location e.g. near school 3. High level of traffic or pedestrians in the vicinity	*** even where not amounting to special reasons**

Appendix 11
Sentencing Guidelines for In Charge Whilst Unfit Through Drink or Drugs

Unfit through drink or drugs (in charge)	Road Traffic Act 1988, s.4(2)

Triable only summarily:
Maximum: Level 4 fine and/or 3 months

Must endorse and may disqualify. If no disqualification, impose 10 points

Offence seriousness (culpability and harm)
A. Identify the appropriate starting point

Starting points based on first time offender pleading not guilty

Examples of nature of activity	Starting Point	Range
Evidence of moderate level of impairment and no aggravating factors	Band B fine	Band B fine 10 points

Evidence of moderate level of impairment and presence of one or more aggravating factors listed below	Band B fine	Band B fine 10 points or consider disqualification
Evidence of high level of impairment and no aggravating factors	Band C fine	Band C fine to medium level community order 10 points or consider disqualification
Evidence of high level of impairment and presence of one or more aggravating factors listed below	High level community order	Medium level community order to 12 weeks custody Consider disqualification OR 10 points

Offence seriousness (culpability and harm)

B. Consider the effect of aggravating and mitigating factors (other than those within examples above)

Common aggravating and mitigating factors are identified in the pullout card - the following may be particularly relevant but **these lists are not exhaustive**

Factors indicating higher culpability	Factors indicating lower culpability
1. LGV, HGV, PSV, etc 2. High likelihood of driving 3. Driving for hire or reward	1. Low likelihood of driving

Appendix 12
Sentencing Guidelines for Driving with Excess Alcohol

Note for offence committed on/after 12th March 2015
level 5 fines are unlimited

Excess alcohol (drive/ attempt to drive)	Road Traffic Act 1988, s.5(1)(a)

Triable only summarily:
Maximum: Level 5 fine and/or 6 months

- Must endorse and disqualify for at least 12 months
- Must disqualify for **at least** 2 years if offender has had two or more disqualificationsfor periods of 56 days or more in preceeding 3 years
- Must disqualify for **at least** 3 years if offender has been convicted of a relevant offence in preceeding 10 years

If there is a delay in sentencing after conviction, consider interim disqualification

Offence seriousness (culpability and harm)
A. Identify the appropriate starting point

Starting points based on first time offender pleading not guilty

Level of Alcohol

Breath (ug)	Blood (mg)	Urine (mg)	Starting Point	Range	Disqual.	Disqual. 2nd offence in 10 years - see note above
36-59	81-137	108-183	Band C fine	Band C fine	12-16 months	36-40 months
60-89	138-206	184-274	Band C fine	Band C fine	17-22 months	36-46 months
90-119	207-275	275-366	Medium level comm. order	Low level comm. order to high level comm. order	23-28 months	36-52 months
120-150 and above	276-345 and above	367-459 and above	12 weeks custody	High level comm. order to 26 weeks custody	29-36 months	36-60 months

Offence seriousness (culpability and harm)

B. Consider the effect of aggravating and mitigating factors (other than those within examples above)

Common aggravating and mitigating factors are identified in the pullout card - the following may be particularly relevant but **these lists are not exhaustive**

Factors indicating higher culpability	**Factors indicating lower culpability**
1. LGV, HGV, PSV, etc 2. Poor road or weather conditions 3. Carrying passengers 4. Driving for hire or reward 5. Evidence of unacceptable standard of driving	1. Genuine emergency established* 2. Spiked drinks* 3. Very short distance driven* ***even where not amounting to special reasons**
Factors indicating greater degree of harm 1. Involved in accident 2. Location e.g. near school 3. High level of traffic or pedestrians in the vicinity	

Appendix 13
Sentencing Guidelines for in Charge with Excess Alcohol

Excess alcohol (in charge)	Road Traffic Act 1988, s.5(1)(b)

Triable only summarily:
Maximum: Level 4 fine and/or 3 months

Must endorse and may disqualify. If no disqualification, improse 10 points

Offence seriousness (culpability and harm)
A. Identify the appropriate starting point

Starting points based on first time offender pleading not guilty

Level of Alcohol

Breath (ug)	Blood (mg)	Urine (mg)	Starting Point	Range
36-59	81-137	108-183	Band B fine	Band B fine 10 points
60-89	138-206	184-274	Band B fine	Band B fine
90-119	207-275	275-366	Band C fine	Band C fine to medium level community order Consider disqualification up to 6 months OR 10 points
120-150 and above	276-345 and above	367-459 and above	Medium level community order	Low level community order to 6 weeks custody Disqualify 6-12 months

Offence seriousness (culpability and harm)

B. Consider the effect of aggravating and mitigating factors (other than those within examples above)

Common aggravating and mitigating factors are identified in the pullout card - the following may be particularly relevant but **these lists are not exhaustive**

Factors indicating higher culpability	Factors indicating lower culpability
1. LGV, HGV, PSV, etc 2. Ability to drive seriously impaired 3. High likelihood of driving 4. Driving for hire or reward	1. Low likelihood of driving

Appendix 14
Sentencing Guidelines for Driving Whilst Disqualified

Note for offence committed on/after 12th March 2015
level 5 fines are unlimited

Fail to provide specimen for analysis (drive/ attempt to drive)	Road Traffic Act 1988, s.7(6)

Triable only summarily:
Maximum: Level 5 fine and/or 6 months

• Must endorse and disqualify for at least 12 months
• Must disqualify for **at least** 2 years if offender has had two or more disqualifications for periods of 56 days or more in preceeding 3 years
• Must disqualify for **at least** 3 years if offender has been convicted of a relevant offence in preceeding 10 years

If there is a delay in sentencing after conviction, consider interim disqualification

Note: the final column below provides guidance regarding the length of disqualification that may be appropriate in cases to which the 3 year minimum applies. The period to be imposed in any individual case will depend on an assessment of all the relevant circumstances, including the length of time since the earlier ban was imposed and the gravity of the current offence.

Offence seriousness (culpability and harm)
A. Identify the appropriate starting point

Starting points based on first time offender pleading not guilty

Examples of nature of activity	Starting Point	Range	Dis-qualification	Dis. 2nd offence in 10 years
Defendant refused test when had honestly held but unreasonable excuse	Band C fine	Band C fine	12-16 months	36 to 40 months
Deliberate refusal or deliberate failure	Low level comm. order	Band C fine to high level comm. order	17-28 months	36 to 46 months

Deliberate refusal or deliberate failure where evidence of serious impairment	12 weeks custody	High level comm. order to 26 weeks custody	29-36 months	36 to 60 months

Offence seriousness (culpability and harm)
B. Consider the effect of aggravating and mitigating factors (other than those within examples above)

Common aggravating and mitigating factors are identified in the pullout card - the following may be particularly relevant but **these lists are not exhaustive**

Factors indicating higher culpability	Factors indicating lower culpability
1. Evidence of unacceptable standard of driving 2. LGV, HGV, PSV, etc 3. Obvious state of intoxication 4. Driving for hire or reward	1. Low likelihood of driving
Factor indicating greater degree of harm	
1. Involved in accident	

Appendix 15
Schedule of Parking/ Related Offences and Penalties

Offence	Section	Penalty	Endorsement Disqualifica- tion
Obstruction of the highway	S137 Highways Act 1980	Level 3 £1,000	None
Obstruction of a road	S42 Road Traffic Act 1988	Level 4 £2,5000	None
Obstruction of a Street	S28 Town Police Causes Act 1847	14 day imprisonment/ Level 3 £1,000	None

Contravention of a Traffic regulation order	S5 Road Traffic Regulation Act 1984	Level 3 £1,000	None
Contravention of a Traffic regulation order (Gtr London)	S8 Road Traffic Regulation Act 1984	Level 3 £1,000	None
Contravention of parking places	ss35A(1) $7(1) Road Traffic Regulation Act 1984	Level 2 £500	None
Contravention of parking places reserved for disabled vehicles	ss35A(1) 47 (1) Road Traffic Regulation Act 1984	Level 3 £1,000	None
Improper Use of a disabled badge	S117 Road Traffic Regulation Act 1984	Level 3 £1,000	None

Driving on footpaths, etc	Traffic Act 1988	Level 3 £1,000	None
Illegal parking on verges etc	S19 Road Traffic Act 1988	Level 3 £1,000	None
Immobilising vehicles	S54 pro-tection of Freedoms Act 2012	Cr Ct – Unlimited fine Magistrates Level 5 £5,000	None
Driving on commons	S193(4) Law of Property 1925	Level 1 £200	None
Depositing builders skips illegally on the highway	S139 (1), (3) Highways Act 1980	Level 3 £1,000	None

Negligent opening of doors	S42 Road Traffic Act 1988 Reg 105 Construction and Use Regs	Level 4 £2,500	None
Negligent opening of car doors	S78 Highway Act 1935	Level 1 £200	None
Leaving a car in a dangerous position	S22 Road Traffic Act 1988	Level 3 £1,000	None
Improper parking at night	S43 Road Traffic Act 1988 reg 101 construction and use regs	Level 4 £2,500	None
Parking or driving illegally on cycle track	S161(1) Highways act 1980	Level 3 £1,000	None

Depositing mud on the highway	S161(1) Highways Act 1980	Level 3 £1,000	None
Annoyance by playing games on the highway	S161(3) Highways Act 1980	Level 1 £200	None
Abandoning a vehicle	S2(1) Refuse Disposal (Amenity) Act 1978	Level 3 £1,000 /3 months imprisonment or both	None

Appendix 16
Prosecution Costs
Schedule

These Court costs apply to offences committed on or after the 13th April 2015 and are in addition to the prosecution costs.

Description of Court Hearing	Prosecution Costs
Conviction by a magistrates court in proceedings conducted by single magistrate on the papers	£85
Conviction by a magistrates court for a summary offence on a guilty plea(magistrates only offence)	£105-160

Conviction by magistrates court where a) no plea entered b) tried in absence of the defendant and c) dealt with on papers no oral evidence	£85
Conviction by magistrates court for a triable either-way offence (triable either in the magistrates or the crown court)	£145-£220
Conviction by a magistrates court at a trial for a summary offence	£620-930
Conviction by magistrates court at a trial for a either way offence	£770-£1,150
Conviction by the Crown Court on a guilty plea	£340-£510
Conviction by the Crown Court at trial on Indictment	£2,800 - £4,200
Crown Court dismissing an appeal against conviction or sentence	£260-£620

Index